PRAISE FOR
In the Beginning Was the Word

"This book is more than biblical interpretation. It is poetry — and poetry about the greatest work of poetry ever generated: the Prologue to John's gospel. Anthony Esolen writes with erudition that never encumbers his eloquence. He situates the New Testament text in its Old Testament context, and he calls the saints and sages to witness to the truth and beauty that are obscured in clumsy modern (even official) translations. I closed the book feeling gratitude and awe."

— **SCOTT HAHN**, co-author of *The Decline and Fall of Sacred Scripture: How the Bible Became a Secular Book*

"Anthony Esolen uses the magnifying glass of his vast erudition like a detective to inspect 'the most influential paragraph in the history of man' — the first eighteen verses of the Gospel of John. In a word-by-word commentary that is accessible and scholarly, robustly orthodox, and poetically inspiring, the great translator of Dante sheds new light on St John's meditation on the incarnation and thus opens our eyes and our hearts to the deep truths embedded there."

— **FR DWIGHT LONGENECKER**, author of *Letters on Liturgy*

"Here philological expertise — not only in Greek, but in the Hebrew and Aramaic that underlie it — is brought to bear on the paragraph of text that is arguably the most pregnant with meaning of any ever written. Above all, this exegesis is open to and sensitive to poetry: the poetry of the beloved disciple's love and (even more importantly) the poetry of his Divine Master's teaching, which points us to what is beyond words. The weight, force, and ordering of each word is considered in the context both of John's gospel and of the Bible as a whole. The discussion is informed by a wide awareness of poetry, liturgical texts, and theological thought, but, shining through it all, is love, not just for these words, but for the Word Incarnate — a love that works to open the reader's heart and mind to the Savior."

— **FR LUKE BELL**, author of *The Meaning of Blue: Recovering a Contemplative Spirit*

"Holy Scripture is an inexhaustible source of wisdom even though contemporary translations often render it lifeless and unimaginative. In this splendid gem of a book, Anthony Esolen reminds us that all Scripture — perhaps especially the Gospel of John — sparkles and delights, if only we would see its theological, philosophical, and poetical brilliance. You won't find a better guide than Esolen if you want to understand the beauty of the Good Book."

— R. J. SNELL, author of *Acedia and Its Discontents: Metaphysical Boredom in an Empire of Desire*

"The most famous prologue in the world does not precede its *logos*, but rather articulates it. Herein sounds the Utterance that *made* the world, with vocabulary and meter both logical and lyrical. No one better than a translator of Dante could help us to hear not only the doctrine, but also the poetry, of this Word. Augustine and Aquinas wrote their own marvelous commentaries, but their Latin could not always do justice to the Greek subtleties and the Semitic atmospheres at work in St John's mind. Anthony Esolen here reveals something of the original tongues that fed into this theological overture, allowing our souls to resonate with the allusive overtones of the *Logos* that tells us our Story."

— SCOTT RANDALL PAINE, author of *The Other World We Live In: A Catholic Vision of Angelic Reality*

"*And the Word became flesh.* Standard literary criticism cannot do justice to these all-important words that tower over all others. Anthony Esolen guides us in a sapiential exploration that delves into them as inspired literature, eliciting a profound love for all the particularities of the sacred word. This unique, arresting book allows a mere eighteen verses to shed their light into the very heart of life and culture!"

— R. JARED STAUDT, author of *The Beer Option: Brewing a Catholic Culture Yesterday & Today*

In the Beginning Was the Word

In the Beginning Was the Word

An Annotated Reading of the Prologue of John

By
ANTHONY ESOLEN

Foreword by Peter Kwasniewski

Angelico Press

I dedicate this book
to our long-time pastor,
Father Richard Bucci,
a "workman that needeth
not to be ashamed, rightly
handling the word of truth."

CONTENTS

FOREWORD

Peter Kwasniewski

IN THIS EXTENDED MEDITATION, ANTHONY ESOLEN looks phrase-by-phrase at John 1:1–18, which he calls, and with good reason, "the most influential paragraph in the history of man." His aim is to unfold its theological richness by showing how the Apostle John has in mind not only what he saw Jesus do and heard Him say, but the whole of Scripture before Him, and the way the young Church proclaimed Him. One of the unique contributions of this extended meditation is Esolen's vivid sense of the Hebrew and Aramaic that can be "heard" beneath John's Greek, because John is a native speaker of Aramaic and an Israelite who is composing directly in a language that is not his mother tongue. When you pay close attention to the Greek, which often echoes that of the Septuagint, and perceive the Hebrew/Aramaic underlying it, all at once a text you never thought could be more profoundly moving than it already is bursts into poetic splendor and keen and comprehensive theological insight. Bad translations blunt most of the power, but any translation into English is going to lose a great deal, which Esolen seeks to recover for us.

Both in what he says and in the specifics of the poetic manner in which he says it, St. John seeks to show us *Jesus, the Christ, the Word Incarnate*, so that this Gospel is at once the most intimate of the four, and the one that presents to us a Person infinitely exalted and impossible to understand as a merely human teacher. Esolen's decades-long experience in reading, hearing, and unlocking poetry illuminates what John wishes us to hear. And, when it comes to poetry, John is not the originator: the beloved disciple caught the habit from the Lord Himself.

The author of these sparkling pages leads us into the unfathomable wisdom of the Prologue to the loftiest of biblical books, written by the virgin apostle who alone among the first synod of bishops braved the blood and brawn of Golgotha. Perhaps better than any other Christian in history, St. John teaches us the virtue of restfulness in God. The Beloved Disciple took his time at the Last Supper when leaning on the breast of Jesus; he did not think there were more urgent things to do, be it selling

ointments to get money for the poor, strategizing against the sneaky enemies of his Lord, or even preaching the good news he was later inspired
to write down. No, at the solemn moment when the sacramental Sacrifice
was being instituted, John knew where he had to be and what he had to
be doing: at the side of his Master, in the adoring silence of a friendship
so intimate that it would later spill over in the most sublime revelations
ever vouchsafed to man. John heard his Gospel beating in the Heart of
Jesus, High Priest and Victim; there he learned the meaning of *Eucharistia*.
St. John is therefore the patron not only of theologians but of all who
"worship God in spirit and in truth." He leads us back, again and again, to
the historic liturgies of the Catholic Church, whose seeds the Lord sowed
into the soil of His apostles' souls in the Upper Room.

This Prologue states the essence of our faith and refutes all heresies;[1] it
proclaims in the clearest and boldest terms the Incarnation of the Son of
God, on which our entire religion and its highest form of worship rests.
The Prologue, in addition to stating the foundational truth that Jesus is
the Son of the Father and the Lord of creation, points to the essence of
the Holy Eucharist as the memorial and actualization of Christ's redemptive work.

This Prologue brings into sharp focus the dependency of all being
upon God, upon His divine artistry: "All things were made by Him: and
without Him was made nothing that was made," *omnia per ipsum factum
sunt, et sine ipso factum est nihil, quod factum est* (Jn. 1:3). This throws down
the gauntlet to every kind of idolatry, materialism, or Pelagianism that
could possibly exist. "The chief obstacle to religion is for man to adhere
to a false god."[2] Of special benefit today, it strikes modern technological
scientism at its root. As Charles De Koninck says:

> The limit to which experimental science tends is the condition of
> a demiurge. The method of invention of reasons which anticipate
> experience is a method of reconstruction. In this very precise
> respect considered abstractly, to reconstruct the universe is in
> some way to construct it. And if *per impossibile* this limit could be

---

1   Cf. St. Thomas, *Commentary on the Gospel of John*, trans. F. R. Larcher, O. P. (Lander,
WY: The Aquinas Institute for the Study of Sacred Doctrine, 2013), n. 10: "John the
Evangelist, who had drawn the truth about the divinity of the Word from the very
fountainhead of the divine breast, wrote this Gospel at the request of the faithful. And
in it he gives us the doctrine of the divinity of Christ and refutes all heresies."
2   St. Thomas, *Summa theologiae* II-II, qu. 122, art. 2.

accomplished, the universe would be nothing but a projection of
our own *logoi*.[3]

St. John states, once and for all, as though to destroy in its root this per-
verse tendency of the human intellect to re-create the world: ALL THINGS
were made through Him (namely, the Word, the *Logos*, of God), and without Him was made NOTHING that was made: OMNIA *per ipsum*, NIHIL *sine
ipso*. Nihilism is the denial of this all-encompassing Word through whom
the All was made; Christianity is the acceptance, the passionate embrace,
the adoration, of this Word, and the love for the All which exists through
it and for it. André Gushurst-Moore remarks:

> The Gospel reveals a radiance at the heart of things, a glorious
> shining, the uncreated light of the *logos* which is the opposite of
> the postmodern abyss: there is no emptiness. This is the true light
> that the Enlightenment threatened to banish, and in fact, for many,
> did cast into shadow.[4]

This Prologue shows the intimacy of the Father and the Son — an
intimacy as great as this: "In the beginning was the Word, and the Word
was with God, and the Word was God," In *principio erat Verbum, et Verbum
erat apud Deum, et Deus erat Verbum* (Jn. 1:1). It shows us that this Word is
the principle of our union with God: "In Him was life, and the life was
the light of men. . . . He gave them power to be made the sons of God, to
them that believe in His name" (Jn. 1:4, 12). In *ipso vita erat, et vita erat lux
hominum . . . dedit eis potestatem filios Dei fieri, his qui credunt in nomine eius*. It
reveals, as in the briefest flash, the link between the Name, the Face, and
the Heart. We who believe in His name have seen His glory, the One who
is full of grace and truth: *vidimus gloriam eius . . . plenum gratiae et veritatis*.

This Prologue inserts the mission of the faithful into the center of God's
mystery: "There was a man sent from God, whose name was John. This
man came for a witness." *Fuit homo missus a Deo, cui nomen erat Joannes: hic
venit in testimonium* (Jn. 1:6–7). The prophetic mission of the Baptist who
points out the Lamb of God is our mission, too, as worshipers and followers of the Lamb, who bear testimony to the mystery into which, by divine
mercy, we have been incorporated. To follow the Lamb whithersoever He

---

3 *On the Primacy of the Common Good: Against the Personalists*, trans. Sean Collins, in *The
Aquinas Review*, vol. 4 (1997): 126.

4 *Glory in All Things: Saint Benedict and Catholic Education Today* (Brooklyn, NY: Angelico
Press, 2020), 161.

goeth, straying for no reason, avoiding at all costs a sliding back into the world which, though it was made by Him, does not acknowledge Him: "the world was made by him, and the world knew him not," *mundus per ipsum factus est, et mundus eum non cognovit* (Jn. 1:10). We are being asked to know Him, to be born from God, *ex Deo*, and not by blood, *ex sanguinibus* — not by violence (recall how the liturgy at the Offertory speaks of "the men of blood": *Ne perdas cum impiis, Deus, animam meam, et cum viris sanguinum vitam meam*), not by fleshly desires and satisfactions, *ex voluntate carnis*, not as though we were the source of our redemption and the goal of our beatitude, *ex voluntate viri* — not, in a word, as though we were Pelagians who save ourselves, but solely, humbly, thankfully, gloriously from God, *ex Deo*.

Finally, St. John the Baptist is proclaimed as the one who preached "that all men might believe through him," *ut omnes crederent per illum* (Jn. 1:7). All will believe through his preaching, so that we shall never forget that Jesus Christ came in the flesh at a given moment in history, to a given people, in the most particular of particular circumstances, and that John, as a consequence, is always the one who prepares the way of the Lord for us. We must go to Jesus in the way He chose, that is, by hearing the Baptist's preaching of repentance and turning away from sin. We do not believe in a Cosmic Christ, in some abstraction of Hegelian theology, but in the carpenter's son, the Jew of Nazareth, whose way was prepared by a single wild prophet in the desert. This prophet will always be preaching to the desert of the world, and will always precede Christ with the message of conversion — just as the Epistle precedes and disposes us to the Gospel, in which the Truth Himself teaches us.

Let us sit up and take heed, and join the ranks of those who hear, savor, and live the poetry of God, and let us pray that one day this magnificent Prologue will once again grace the conclusion of the Mass as it had done for a millennium.

Peter A. Kwasniewski
November 1, 2021
The Feast of All Saints

PREFACE

I AM WRITING THIS BOOK TO SET DOWN MY THOUGHTS
upon one short text, the first eighteen verses of John's gospel. I believe
that it is the most significant short piece of writing in the history of
the world. That claim, even if one does not accept it, should be no more
controversial than if I had said that Dante is the world's greatest poet, or
that Michelangelo is the world's greatest sculptor. It is certainly a defen-
sible claim. Yet the very significance of this text, looming before us like
a giant, can cause us to overlook features that are small and near, and yet
that are essential to its meaning and power.

Christian iconographers have for many centuries illustrated this gospel
with the figure of the eagle, one of the four beasts of the Apocalypse,
six-winged and filled with eyes, that "rest not day and night, saying, Holy,
holy, holy, Lord God Almighty, which was, and is, and is to come" (4:8). It
is well that they should do so, because John, the eagle of God, the "disciple
whom Jesus loved" (Jn. 13:23 and *passim*), as he so meekly calls himself,
saw most deeply into the heart of the Lord. God cannot be grasped by the
intellect, says the anonymous author of *The Cloud of Unknowing*; only love
can grasp him. Where there is love, there is an eye, says Richard of Saint
Victor. Love opens the eyes, and God is ready to make himself known to
those who love him. "He that hath my commandments," says Jesus, "and
keepeth them, he it is that loveth me: and he that loveth me shall be loved
of my Father, and I will love him, and will manifest myself to him" (Jn.
14:21). John loved, and he saw.

But let us come to earth again. This text is the more remarkable for
something so obvious it is embarrassing to mention it. If I were to recite
a powerful passage from Dante, let us say the prologue to his *Paradiso*, I
might feel that strange shiver we feel in the presence of the artistically
sublime, as is fitting for *la gloria di colui chi tutto move* — *the glory of the One
who moves all things*. The poetry might take me by storm, but it would not
exactly surprise me. Why should it? Dante is a great poet writing in the
medium he has worked with all his life, the Italian language. Or think of
Michelangelo and his art. To glance at the sober countenance of Joseph
of Arimathea, Michelangelo's own in his middle age, as he and Mary and

xvii

Mary Magdalene try to bear up the body of Jesus as they take him down from the cross, is to see what fifty years of touch can do, the hand on the chisel, the file, and the marble, when you are that great sculptor and you have loved that medium all your life. But John?

John is not the greatest writer of Greek in the New Testament. That is Saint Luke, whose first language is Greek, or it is Paul of Tarsus, fluent in it, and muscular. Even Matthew and Mark have this advantage over John, that they are composing in their native Aramaic and then working it up into Greek, or having it translated for them. But John is composing straight into Greek, which is not native to him.

And more: I believe he is composing *poetically*. I do not mean that John uses plenty of metaphors and figures of speech. He is sparing of those, and such figures of speech as we find in him are not his to begin with. They are the Lord's, and the beloved disciple has long dwelt upon them. I mean that John has in mind the forms of Hebrew poetry. That habit too he catches from Jesus. For Jesus, as I believe, has composed luminous and memorable poetry, in Aramaic or Hebrew, in his great prayer to the Father, in the Beatitudes, and in many of his sayings.

Now, we cannot expect John to compose Greek poetry in Greek forms. It would be like asking a guitar player to compose a fugue for the organ. The so-called quantitative meters of Greek are appropriate for a language with words of many syllables, with those syllables distinctly long and short in duration and discretely pronounced. The Greek meters are wholly foreign to English with its strong and fixed patterns of stress, let alone to a language like Hebrew, with its terseness, its paucity of prefixes and suffixes that in Greek make for long and melodious words, and its so-called "schwa," the hardly pronounced vowel that makes it difficult, and perhaps irrelevant, to say just how many syllables a word has. So the evangelist handles Greek words as if they were Hebrew words, stark blocks of meaning set one beside or against the other, simple words of elemental significance: life, light, darkness, bread, blood, water, flesh, world, truth, glory. The poetry is conveyed not by his skill in the Greek medium, and indeed he lays claim to none, but by those elements, robed adventitiously in Greek garb, but always themselves. We translate less from John's Greek into English than from those elements into thought and vision.

Some discussion here is in order, I think, regarding how different John's gospel is from the so-called synoptic gospels of Matthew, Mark, and Luke, and from the letters of Saint Paul.

First, I will often take the opportunity to show that John and the others are saying the same things in different ways, and this is especially true when we compare the gospel of John with the letters of Paul. We should be struck by any similarity between John and Paul, because at first glance — but only at first glance — it is hard to imagine two personalities farther apart than that of the apparently — apparently! — soft and tender John, and that of the apparently — apparently! — brusque and hard-edged Paul. John is the mystic, and Paul is the moral theologian. So we might say, and then we would be brought up short by reality, more interesting and intricate than our scholarly reductions. For Saint Paul is the mystic who said, referring gingerly to himself, "I knew a man in Christ above fourteen years ago (whether in the body, I cannot tell; or whether out of the body, I cannot tell: God knoweth), such an one caught up to the third heaven" (2 Cor. 12:2). And Saint John is the fiery preacher who will not compromise with bad feelings, let alone with bad deeds: "Whosoever hateth his brother is a murderer; and ye know that no murderer hath eternal life abiding within him" (1 Jn. 3:15).

Second, I believe that the uniqueness of John's gospel has at least one obvious and proximate cause. If John wrote after the other gospels had been written, why would he repeat what had already been recorded in the others? As Dorothy Sayers pointed out in *The Whimsical Christian*, we have almost no public preaching in John. Instead we have the words of Jesus to his most intimate circle of disciples, or to very small delegations of Jewish leaders, or to a single person such as Nicodemus, in a private setting (Jn. 3). Which of us speaks publicly the same way he speaks privately? Publicly, Jesus preaches the new law of charity, in memorable form, that is, in poetry (the Beatitudes, the Lord's Prayer), and in his inimitable parables; and these, it is easy to imagine, Jesus preached many times over the course of three years, on the side of a high hill, as Matthew records (5:1), and on a plain, as Luke records (6:17), and likely in plenty of other places too, where large crowds could hear him at once. In his preaching, Jesus, speaking with authority, *implies* rather than reveals outright who he is. What else could we imagine he should do? Proclaim to a multitude, including many pagans, that he was the son of God? Embroil himself in a controversy over what was the true bread from heaven? The people first needed the path that would lead to him. But to those whom he could address in private, directly, he could say, "I AM the way, and the truth, and the life" (Jn. 14:6).

This second point implies a third. Just as the *matter* of public and private speaking will differ, so will the *manner*. Therefore we should not follow the lead of scholars who suppose that the words of Jesus that John records must be less reliable than are the words that the other evangelists record, just because a cursory reading shows that John's style is not their style. And as far as that style is concerned, we must remember that John is composing directly from his memory into what is not his native language. If you ever have occasion to do such a thing, you will find yourself narrowing your vocabulary and keeping your grammatical constructions simple. You will have to rely upon fewer nouns and fewer verbs, mainly those stalwarts that every speaker knows, and your adjectives will be even fewer. You will also rely upon repetition. Listen to any homilist from Haiti speaking to an American congregation, and you will have the experience that the Haitians themselves have, when an American priest comes to them with his workmanlike French.

Such simplicity will make it so much the more impressive and telling, when the homilist, leaving for a moment the homiletic, attempts to describe a scene, the where and when and how something happened. And then he is compelled to search for a few words to name the humble things around us.

That is exactly what Saint John does, and he does it all the time. He is the eyewitness. So he mentions the fig tree and Nathanael (1:48), the six stone jars at Cana, and their size (2:6), Jacob's well (4:5), the pool of Bethesda near the sheep market (5:1), Philip — amiable and slow-witted Philip — estimating how much it would cost to feed the people (6:7), how many furlongs they were out on the sea when the storm came (6:19), how Jesus traced letters on the ground when the woman was caught in adultery (8:6), how he spat on the ground and made a mud paste to press into the eyes of the blind man (9:6), the nervous evasions of the blind man's parents (9:21), how Jesus delayed when he heard that his friend Lazarus was dying (11:6), Martha's embarrassment when Jesus orders the tomb to be opened (11:39), Lazarus's appearance, "his face bound about with a napkin" (11:44), Judas's estimation of how much the spikenard would cost (12:5), the palm branches the people lay before Jesus as he entered Jerusalem (12:13), how Jesus undressed and girt himself with a towel, to wash the disciples' feet (13:4), how Jesus dipped his bread into the sauce when Judas did the same (13:26), the name of the servant whose ear Peter cut off, when Jesus was seized by the guard (18:10), the charcoal fire where Peter warmed himself (18:18), the tense conversation with the jaded Pilate, who said exactly what a Roman of his sort would say, "What is truth?" (18:38), the soldiers casting dice for Jesus's cloak (19:24), the soldiers breaking the legs of those who were crucified alongside Jesus, to bring about immediate death (19:32; it is death by asphyxiation, because the men would no longer be able to lift themselves a little to expand the chest and get a gulp of air), the lance the soldier thrust through Jesus's side, into the lungs and heart — filled with fluid from congestive heart failure, so that "forthwith came there out blood and water" (19:34), the great weight of the myrrh and aloes that Nicodemus brought to anoint Jesus's body (19:39), the race to the empty tomb, and who outran whom (20:4), Mary Magdalen's mistaking the risen Jesus for the gardener (20:15), Jesus's taking Thomas by the hand to probe his wounds (20:27), and the fishing at the sea of Tiberias (21:3).

Many of these accounts include details that we recognize as what a man seizes upon, years later, not because his hearers know what he is talking about, but because they help bring the whole scene to his mind. (We all do that. I can recall getting ready for Mass when I was a small boy, by thinking about the shoe polish we kept in a cupboard underneath the kitchen sink.) Tradition has it that John wrote his gospel in Ephesus, on the coast of Asia Minor, far away from Judea, and so he might well find his memories of Jesus bound up with memories of a hill here, a pool there.

Did John include such details to lend credence to his account? The question would make no sense to him or to his readers. It would be seventeen hundred years before journalism would be invented, and eighteen hundred years before the realistic novel. Nobody expected such things. They are bells for John, not for the faraway Greeks in Ephesus to whom he preached. That does not mean that we should ignore them. The details are incidental, but they can assume great meaning even for those who have never seen the village of Bethany or a watering-place in Samaria. In our minds, they give to John's witness a local habitation and a name. We can see then why Christians would be so eager to do what was new in the Mediterranean world: to go on a holy pilgrimage, to find the places where Jesus lived and taught, and worked his wonders, and suffered and died and rose again.

My fourth point is that it is easy to exaggerate the stylistic differences between John and the Synoptics. Consider the following passage from the Sermon on the Mount, quite Semitic in its playing on the grammar of single verbs:

> Judge not, that ye be not judged.
> For with what judgment ye judge, ye shall be judged: and
> with what measure ye mete, it shall be measured to you again.
> (Mt. 7:1–2)

That habit of ringing changes on a repeated word is prominent throughout John's gospel, for example in Jesus's high priestly prayer:

> I have glorified thee on the earth: I have finished the work which
> thou gavest me to do.
> And now, O Father, glorify thou me with thine own self with
> the glory which I had with thee before the world was. (Jn. 17:4–5)

Or think of the Semitic affinity for stark but surprising contrasts, often involving an ironic reversal of expectations:

> If any man will come after me, let him deny himself, and take up
> his cross, and follow me.
> For whosoever will save his life shall lose it; and whosoever will
> lose his life for my sake shall find it. (Mt. 16:24–25)

So, in John's gospel, Jesus speaks to the angry Pharisees after he has healed the blind man:

> For judgment I am come into the world, that they which see not
> might see; and that they which see might be made blind.
> And some of the Pharisees which were with him heard these
> words, and said unto him, Are we blind also?
> Jesus said unto them, If ye were blind, ye should have no sin:
> but now ye say, We see; therefore your sin remaineth. (Jn. 9:39–41)

Or think of the extended similes that Jesus uses to teach the people in words they could not forget, using images from the directly perceived objects of ordinary life, yet broaching such mysteries that no man ever shall come near to fathoming their depths:

> The kingdom of heaven is like to a grain of mustard seed, which
> a man took, and sowed in his field.
> Which indeed is the least of all seeds, but when it is grown, it
> is the greatest among herbs, and becometh a tree, so that the birds
> of the air come and lodge in the branches thereof. (Mt. 13:31–32)

Now see Jesus, in the gospel of John, applying the same kinds of similes not to the kingdom of heaven, but to his own person and mission:

> I am the good shepherd: the good shepherd giveth his life for
> the sheep.
> But he that is an hireling, and not the shepherd, whose own
> the sheep are not, seeth the wolf coming, and leaveth the sheep,
> and fleeth: and the wolf catcheth them, and scattereth the sheep.
> The hireling fleeth, because he is an hireling, and careth not
> for the sheep.
> I am the good shepherd, and know my sheep, and am known
> of mine. (Jn. 10:11–14)

Here someone may say shift his tactics, and grumble not about the differences, but about the *similarities*, saying that a clever impostor might introduce such into his writing to pass off his work as genuine. I have already said that journalistic details add no credibility when there is no such thing as journalism. But beyond that, scattering their work with them is exactly what clever impostors *do not do*. It does not occur to them to do it, because they shy away from such things as irrelevant to the task at hand. Precise details are like great rocks of reality on the seacoast, threatening to rip the hull out of your ship if you draw too near, because you do not really know what the rocks are or where they are. What would be the point of mentioning the name of a pool, when you are hundreds of miles away and almost nobody reading your words would know what you were talking about?

Then there are the stylistic *similarities*. The critics must now make up their minds. They cannot say in one breath that John is less reliable than are the other three evangelists because his gospel is quite different from theirs, and then say in the next breath that he must have cribbed from them various habits of Jesus's speech. We may call this the fallacy of damning-both-ways. The book of Revelation, we are told, is not John's because such themes as love and grace are not prominent in it, as they are in his gospel and his letters. Whether the themes are not prominent in it because they were not prominent in the actual vision the apostle was granted, they do not ask, because they most likely do not believe that he had the vision to begin with. Meanwhile, the epistle to the Ephesians, the same kinds of scholars say, is *not* Paul's because the author *has* deliberately included Pauline imagery in it, such as that of the full armor of God. [5] If it walks like a duck, it must be a pigeon.

---

5   See Eph. 6:10–17; cf. Rom. 13:12, 2 Cor. 6:7, 1 Th. 5:8.

The obvious answer to the problem is that *there is no problem.* John is aware of the other gospels, but he is writing a different gospel, recalling different incidents and sayings. As for the similarities, the habits of Jesus's speech in John's gospel are like the habits of Jesus's speech in the other gospels, because it was the same person, Jesus, who said what he said.

But could the apostles have written any of the things attributed to them at all? I have long sensed a certain snobbishness among people who assume that ignorant fishermen — for fishermen are always igno-rant — could not conceivably have written well. Would it make matters better if we called Peter the chief executive of a fishing concern? There is no reason to suppose that there could not have been men of extraordi-nary intelligence among the apostles. What work would you do in Judea if you were a boy genius? Most likely you would do what your father did. Again, the critics must really make up their minds, whether we are to regard the apostles as fiendishly clever impostors, or ignorant dupes, because they cannot be both at once.

Let me continue with the charge of imposture. It is to be ruled out for two clear reasons. The first reason is that the whole of Jesus's teaching is founded upon truth and a love for the truth. It is utterly incoherent — we would have to believe in a mass psychopathology, unpersuasive and self-destructive — to have people telling lies in order to preach the Sav-ior who said that Satan is a liar and the father of lies. Liars weasel out of their lies whenever they can, as confidence-men have always done, but the disciples of Jesus would sooner lay down their lives in most horrible and ignominious ways rather than turn their yes into no and their no into yes.

The second reason is rooted in the person and the words of Jesus him-self. Jesus is the most *living* man from history, and no one else comes close. His words are at once apparently simple, so that they can be apprehended by children, but fearfully intricate and infinitely suggestive, so that the greatest minds among us, whether they believe or do not believe, do not dare to say that they understand them through and through. That is as much as to say that the apostles did not impersonate Christ, because *nobody can impersonate Christ.* The addle-pated fellow who cobbled together the so-called Gospel of Thomas could not come within a million miles of it. When he or whoever taught him tries to put a new parable on the lips of Jesus, we get things like this:

> Jesus said, "The kingdom of the father is like a certain man who wanted to kill a powerful man. In his own house he drew his

sword and stuck it into the wall in order to find out whether his
hand could carry through. Then he slew the powerful man." (98)

That sounds as much like Jesus as a dog banging the keys of a toy piano
sounds like Paderewski. When the blockhead tries to mimic the profundity
of Jesus's sayings, such as that where the heart is, there our treasure shall
be also (Mt. 6:21), we get gibberish:

> Jesus said, "He who has recognized the world has found the body,
> but he who has found the body is superior to the world." (80)

That, and a long drag on a roll of hashish, will bring you enlightenment.

It has been two thousand years, and everywhere you beat a bush you
can scare up a dozen poets, but not one among all those talents has ever
composed a parable of such unfathomable simplicity as that of the Prodigal
Son. "A book of riddles" is what Chesterton called the gospel. Who could
have woven it? Not even the wisest of philosophers, said Chesterton:

> A man reading the Gospel sayings would not find platitudes. If he
> had read even in the most respectful spirit the majority of ancient
> philosophers and of modern moralists, he would appreciate the
> unique importance of saying that he did not find platitudes. It is
> more than can be said even of Plato. It is much more than can be
> said of Epictetus or Seneca or Marcus Aurelius or Apollonius of
> Tyana. And it is immeasurably more than can be said of most of
> the agnostic moralists and preachers of the ethical societies; with
> their songs of service and their religion of brotherhood.[6]

Who but Jesus ever could show us the spiritual peril of the elder brother,
who trembles in anger upon the brink of his own salvation or damnation
and does not know it?

Grant that John was no impostor. Could he have been an ignorant and
credulous dupe? That was the line that the nineteenth century skeptics
took. Scholarship is a prophylactic against credulity. But is it, really?
Not if we examine the history of the past century, or the current fads
of madness in our universities. People in the intellectual professions are
usually the first to be fooled: they can reason their way into lies. Who but
a comfortably padded and insulated professor could believe that women
en masse could make soldiers as well as men? Who else could believe that
socialism could eliminate human ambition, envy, and greed? But Peter

---

6   From "The Riddles of the Gospel," in *The Everlasting Man*.

and Andrew and James and John plied a trade that demanded attention to realities. You could not theorize your way around a dangerous body of water like the Sea of Galilee. You must know about wood, pitch, nets, fish, clouds, wind, rain, season, time of day. More than your livelihood, your life depended on it.

And the teaching of Jesus also was grounded in reality. Jesus did not talk in high abstractions about form and matter, and essence and existence. He talked about a widow giving a penny to the Temple treasury. He talked about seed falling among thorns. He talked about a man beaten half to death along the treacherous road from Jerusalem to Jericho. He was utterly shrewd, we might venture to say cynical, about the motives of the rulers of men. He noticed the lilies of the field, but he was not so romantic as to forget that they would be thrown into the oven after a day. To follow Jesus was to become more real, not less; more sane, more aware that even on your best days you are not very good; less apt to accept the slogans of the time; more apt to become like a little child, but with the wisdom of age. These supposedly ignorant apostles of his were about to transform the world.

Grant, then, that John was neither an impostor nor a dupe. Was he John? He had to be someone, and the unanimous testimony of the earliest Christians, and his suggestive reticence regarding his own name, leave us with no good reason to suppose that it was not he.

I am aware that for more than a hundred years, Biblical scholars have been attempting to ascribe, or to deny, apostolic authorship to various books of the New Testament. All such attempts can never be more than sheer guesswork. Do skeptics never consult a mirror? Some skepticism about the skeptics is in order. So long as two letters or two narratives are written in the same language from the same historical period and in the same dialect, there is no way, none, that anyone can say for certain that they were *not* written by the same person. We have no sure method, none, for separating authors.

Had we such a method, we could apply it to authors we know of, with complete reliability. I am thinking now of two plays written around 1600. One of them is a slight bourgeois romantic comedy, written almost entirely in prose. What little poetry it has, is undistinguished. The other is a tragedy of astonishing power, with nervous and sinewy verse, whose prose is more poetic than is the poetry of that comedy. If the authors of each play were anonymous, there is no way that anyone, following the reasoning of Biblical scholars, would attribute the two plays to the same man. Nevertheless, Shakespeare not only wrote both *The Merry Wives of Windsor* and *King Lear*; he wrote them at nearly the same time, one on top of the other. There is almost nothing madcap about *A Tale of Two Cities*, and nothing of grim political seriousness about *The Pickwick Papers*, yet Charles Dickens wrote them both. Here we have novels hundreds of pages long. If we have no reliable test for such things, we should not begin to pretend we can tell anything certain about letters, or about short narrative accounts from which the author and his personality fade into the background. I will assume therefore that the apostle Paul wrote all the letters attributed to him, and — though I will not here insist upon it — that John wrote not only his gospel and epistles, but the book of Revelation too.

What expertise can I myself claim, interpreting John, and for direct commentary limiting myself to the first eighteen verses of the first chapter? I am not a theologian, I have not studied the Johannine manuscripts, I am no great Hebraist. But the unfortunate severance of the humanities one from the other has given us thousands of scholars who study texts that are poetic, though they do not know poetry. The translators of many modern Bibles, including the lethally drab New American Bible, the one I and my fellow Roman Catholics in the United States must hear at Mass, seem to have made all poetry and sublimity their enemies. [7] Perhaps that is one reason why they make baldly confident claims about who must or must not have been the author of a line or a passage or a letter or a gospel, claims that any poet, thinking of the range of poetry he has known and cherished from any single pen, would find exaggerated and perhaps absurd. Meanwhile they miss the song before them. I know poetry. Not Hebrew or Greek but *poetic language and poetic form* are my métiers. And I love the gospel and believe in it.

That is why I am writing this book.

---

7   The minority of Catholics who assist at the traditional Latin Mass are hearing the English of the sixteenth-century Douay-Rheims or a slightly modernized version of it when the readings are read out before the sermon. These congregants are spared the pain of the New American Bible.

1

In the beginning was the Word.

At the Name of Jesus
   every knee shall bow,
Every tongue confess him
   King of glory now;
'Tis the Father's pleasure
   we should call him Lord,
Who from the beginning
   was the mighty Word.[1]

"IN THE BEGINNING WAS THE WORD." SO BEGINS the Gospel of John, the last of the four gospels to be written, and the most exalted and meditative of them all. Catholics who attend the Mass written in the wake of the second Vatican Council will hear these words only once or at most a few times each year—at the Mass "during the day" on Christmas, at the Second Sunday after Christmas, and on the seventh day of the Christmas octave. When it is read by other Christians, I do not know. For a long time, the so-called prologue, verses 1–18, was called "the Last Gospel," because it was read after the dismissal at every Mass. Thus would the people leave having heard not only some things that Jesus said, but who Jesus *was*: and thus might the temptation be checked, to patronize Jesus, to humiliate Him by exalting Him to the status of a great teacher, a deeply spiritual man, an advocate for the poor and the insulted and the injured, and an icon of peaceful resistance against evil.[2]

Says C. S. Lewis in a famous passage:

> You can shut Him up for a fool, you can spit at Him and kill Him as a demon; or you can fall at His feet and call Him Lord and God. But let us not come with any patronizing nonsense about

---

1 Caroline Maria Noel, 1870.

2 This Last Gospel has been returned to its place of honor for Catholics who encounter it weekly or even daily when they attend the older form of the Mass, celebrated anew in many places.

His being a great human teacher. He has not left that open to us.
He did not intend to.[3]

But the Gospel of John is "last" in another sense, one that binds it to the
last book of the New Testament, the Apocalypse — Revelation as we call
it, the unveiling of "things hidden from the foundation of the world." In
the Apocalypse, Jesus testifies to himself as the Alpha and the Omega, the
first and the last, he who was, who is, and who is to come, the everlasting
God. Everything that can be said is included in the alphabet between
Alpha, the first letter, and Omega, the last letter. The ancient hymnodists
were powerfully moved by that consideration, which gave them a way to
approach, though not to comprehend, all things visible and invisible. So
the first great Christian poet, Prudentius (348 – 413), composes a hymn
that binds the eternal begetting of the Son with creation, with his incarnation and nativity, and with all that shall be in time to come and in the
time after time:

> Of the Father's love begotten,
>   Ere the worlds began to be,
> He is Alpha and Omega,
>   He the source, the ending he,
> Of all things that are, that have been,
>   And that future years shall see,
> Evermore and evermore.[4]

In Christ are all things consummated, and from Him all things live and
move and have their being, as sprung from the originating fountain. We
can say *additional* things about Christ, but we cannot say *more*.

I shall not say more. I struggle to say what little I can: to use Dante's
image, when he stands in the presence of God, I am like a baby "who wets
his tongue still at his mother's breast."

How is the Omega implied in the Alpha, unless the Alpha and Omega
are one? We must think of them not as the first and final terms in a
series, but as the same reality manifest under different forms: as the
fount of being, and its aim and perfection. The kingdom of God is both
the mustard seed and the tree in which the birds build their homes. The
locution from the Apocalypse, "the Alpha and the Omega," will help us
understand what John is doing at the beginning of his gospel, and his

---

3   *Mere Christianity*, ch. 3: "What Christians Believe."
4   *Corde natus ex Parentis*, tr. John Mason Neale, 1854, Henry W. Baker, 1859.

comprehensive range. The other evangelists begin at other beginnings, but John's beginning embraces, comprehends them all.

I do not mean to suggest that Matthew, Mark, and Luke begin their gospels adventitiously or without deep theological import. Mark begins with the bold statement: "The beginning of the gospel of Jesus Christ, the Son of God." English, usually rich in words, disappoints us here. The Greek brings out the boldness of it: *Genesis evangeliou Iesou Christou, hyiou Theou.* The first word is *Genesis:* the Greek name for the first book of the Old Testament. Matthew is similar: "The book of the generation of Jesus Christ, the Son of David, the son of Abraham." Again, English misleads us, even the literal translation of the Douay-Rheims which I have just cited. For that word *generation* is *geneseos,* the genitive case for the noun *genesis;* and all the begetting that follows, from Abraham to Jacob the father of Joseph the husband of Mary, is marked by the verb *egennesen,* as we might say, awkwardly, *was the genesis of.* Even when Matthew is about to tell us of the birth of Jesus, he has in mind the begetting, the genesis, and not just the child's delivery from the womb: "Now thus was the genesis of Jesus the Anointed One" (Mt. 1:18; translation mine). Matthew clearly refers both to the genealogy of Jesus that he has recounted, and the conception which he is about to recount. Saint Luke does not use the same words, but his genealogy takes us back from Jesus to "Adam of God," the man made by the very hand of the Most High (Lk. 3:38; translation mine).

We hear in Luke's words the teachings of the great apostle whom he accompanied, Saint Paul, for whom the Anointed is the new Adam, in whom all the saved are engrafted, as onto a new root, a new foundation of being: "For as in Adam all die, even so in Christ shall all be made alive" (1 Cor. 15:22). Paul has no abstraction in mind, but the springs of life: "The first man Adam was made a living soul; the last Adam was made a quickening spirit" (1 Cor. 15:45). Adam was made, *egeneto,* and so he became a soul possessing life, but Christ in the spirit is *zoopoios, life-making,* as God made all things in the beginning. Christ is the image, the *eikon,* that which we behold, "of the invisible God, the firstborn of every creature," says Paul in the fire of theological lyricism, as if he were wrestling with the angel of language itself. "For by him were all things created, that are in heaven, and that are in earth, visible and invisible, whether they be thrones, or dominions, or principalities, or powers: all things were created by him, and for him: and he is before all things, and by him all things consist" (Col. 1:15–17). We see that Paul and John, the storm of fire and the calm

3

immensity of the sea, speak as one. "Behold, I make all things new," says He who sits upon the throne in the Apocalypse (Rev. 21:5). Paul spoke of God's saving work in the same vein, as the full and ultimate making of things forever new: "Therefore if any man be in Christ, he is a new creature: old things are passed away; behold, all things are become new" (2 Cor. 5:17).

What do we make of such a claim about Christ? I have heard many an unbeliever say that the story of Jesus is but the story of every semi-divine hero in the history of the world. That is not true. Quite the contrary. Let us pause to look at the matter.

Alexander the Great traveled all the way to the oasis of Siwah in Libya to consult the oracle of Ammon, whom the Greeks associated with Zeus. He wanted to say that he was the son of Ammonian Zeus, and not the son of the half-barbarian warlord Philip of Macedon, whom, historians believe, Alexander's ambitious mother Olympias put out of her son's path by assassination. Alexander wanted to stamp his aristocratic card. It is an acknowledged trick of the self-promoter, and the ancients themselves saw it as such. The Julian clan in Rome traced their lineage back to Iulus, the son of that Aeneas who, according to old self-promoting Roman folklore, settled his refugees from Troy upon the Italian shores. This Aeneas was the son of Anchises by the goddess Venus. Every important clan wanted a ticket like that. It is like establishing your membership in the Daughters of the American Revolution.

The Pharaohs in Egypt were considered the earthly personifications of the benevolent god of justice, Osiris, guaranteeing the healthy flooding of the Nile, so that people could cast their seed broadside and the bumper crops would come. The Egyptians believed that divine power flowed through the Pharaoh, sure enough, but no one would say of Tutankhamen the boy-king that he was *in himself* the origin of the universe, and its significance. There are many stories in human lore about heroes who rise from obscurity and neglect to the heights of glory. Beowulf is one, but Beowulf dies in the end, and the smoke rises above his funeral pyre and is swallowed up in the sky, while the Geats he ruled look forward to annihilation at the hands of the Swedes, their old enemies. The world is also full of stories of men who achieve enlightenment, which they then pass along to their followers: Socrates, Buddha, Confucius, Lao-Tzu, Zoroaster, even Longfellow's pleasant Hiawatha. Not one of them takes upon his shoulders the sins of the world. Not one of them is or claims to be the Lord of the world.

There is, in the story of Jesus, no sense that he *gains* enlightenment, no dramatic turning point that puts his life on the path to glory. He is not ever the Prince Siddhartha under the Bodhi tree. He is not ever Mohammed, hitherto an ordinary man working among the caravans, visited by a reciting angel in a cave. We have only one account of his boyhood, whence we gather that he was already that same Jesus we know, calmly confident, speaking and listening and replying. There is in his story nothing of Napoleon or Dick Whittington or Epictetus or Oedipus or Arthur or even Moses. The story of Jesus is not like the story of man. It is instead *the key that opens the story of man.* It brings those stories into the light, for all men, and for each man. "I am the door of the sheep," says the Lord. "I am the door: by me if any man enter in, he shall be saved, and shall go in and out, and shall find pasture" (Jn. 10:7, 9). Jesus does not conform his story to ours, but we may find the answers to our stories in his: "If any man hear my voice, and open the door, I will come in to him, and will sup with him, and he with me" (Rev. 3:20).

And so Saint John brings us back to "the beginning," but what does that mean? Let us consider what he surely has in mind, and what he expects those who hear him to have in mind if they are Jews: "In the beginning, God created the heavens and the earth." The Hebrew for that word — for we must remember that John was himself a Jew, thinking first in his native Aramaic and then in the sacred parent language of Hebrew, but writing in his third language, Greek — is *bereshith*, at the *rosh* or the *head* of things. I believe that it meant more to the Jewish mind than our *first* means to us, or *at the start*, or *to begin with*, or even *in the beginning*, if we think of *beginning* only in a temporal sense, for instance as the first domino to fall in a series.

We should not allow our digital clocks and calendars to mislead us. When the Jews celebrated the feast that marked the end of the old year and the beginning of the new, it was not like what Americans do when they gather in Times Square to watch a conglomeration of electric lights "fall," and the numerals change on the historical odometer, whereupon everyone takes a drink, and wakes up the next morning foggy and disillusioned. Says God to Moses: "Thou shalt observe the feast of tabernacles," that is, of barns, granaries, vats, "seven days, after that thou hast gathered in thy corn and thy wine: and thou shalt rejoice in thy feast, thou, and thy son, and thy daughter, and thy manservant, and thy maidservant, and the Levite, the stranger, and the fatherless, and the widow, that are within

5

thy gates. Seven days shalt thou keep a solemn feast unto the Lord thy God in the place which the Lord thy God shall choose: because the Lord thy God shall bless thee in all thine increase, and in all the works of thine hands, therefore shalt thou surely rejoice" (Dt. 16:13–15).

Seven, of course, is the number of days in the week, and the week is the divine unit of time. It is suggested by the lunar month of roughly four weeks, but otherwise it is not observable, not evident to the eye. If I may stretch a point: the week is like the angels, *invisible*. We have the week by the memory of what God has done *in the beginning*: "And on the seventh day God ended his work which he had made; and he rested on the seventh day from all the work which he had made. And God blessed the seventh day, and sanctified it" (Gen. 2:2–3). For that reason they who worship Him must also keep the day holy, "for in six days the Lord made the heaven and earth, the sea, and all that in them is, and rested the seventh day: wherefore the Lord blessed the seventh day, and hallowed it" (Ex. 20:11). We in our anti-culture of work that makes many a bad thing and unmakes many a man and woman, and of hedonism that brings no pleasure, are apt to view the command as a prohibition: do no work on the Sabbath. It is better viewed as an invitation: *Thou shalt feast!* Rest, here, is not simply an interruption in labor. It is the feast, the refreshment, the crown of life. The heavens and the earth and all that is in them are oriented toward the feast. It is the feast that is their root and trunk and crown, their sap and leaf and flower. In the beginning and in the end, there is the feast.

But John, as I have said, though he might think in Aramaic and pray and read the Scriptures in Hebrew, wrote in Greek. The people in Ephesus, where several reliable sources say he went to live and preach, spoke the Greek that in the eastern provinces of the Roman empire was common to travelers, merchants, soldiers, Roman officials, and educated people. Many Jews, who had long been scattered across the Mediterranean world, were native speakers of this Greek; Saul of Tarsus was one. Two of Jesus's apostles had Greek names, not Hebrew: Andrew (Greek *Andreas, manly*), and Philip (Greek *Philippos, lover of horses*), and the name of the blind man cured by Jesus combined a Greek root with the Hebrew prefix Bar-, *Son of*: Bartimaeus, *Son of Timaeus*. Therefore it seems easy to believe that John could read some Greek. His words, in Greek, echo the beginning of the Greek translation of the Old Testament, the Septuagint (LXX):

> En arche en ho logos.
> En arche epoiesen ho Theos ton ouranon kai ten gen.

Does the Greek influence go farther? Many commentators say that John has adopted a powerful word from Greek philosophy, *logos*, to name Christ our Lord. Philo of Alexandria, the cosmopolitan Jewish philosopher, had already used the term *logos* to denote the natural moral law, which he saw as embodied most perfectly in the Mosaic law, many of whose ritual and liturgical requirements he interpreted allegorically. There is no doubt that Philo's methods had considerable though indirect influence upon Christian writers in the churches of north Africa, especially in Alexandria. I will come to that word soon, but here I wish to look at the *first* Greek term John has adopted here, rich in significance. It is *arche*. Again, our English translations have *beginning*, and that will have to do. It is the closest we can come. But *arche* means more than that.

The ancient Greek philosophers, long before Socrates, asked themselves what was the *arche* of the universe. They did not mean the *beginning* in time, not strictly speaking. Thales said that the *arche* was water, because water can assume the three states of matter, solid, liquid, and gas, and because water, ever flowing, seemed the best candidate for the fundamental material of a world in which nothing ever stays the same. For somewhat similar reasons, Heraclitus said that the *arche* was fire. This is what the author of the *Epistle to Diognetus* (2nd c.) had in mind, saying that before the coming of Christ, "who among mankind had any notion at all of what God is? Or do you accept the vapid and ludicrous suggestions of your own pretentious philosophers — some of whom assume that God is Fire . . . some say that He is Water, and others one of the other various elements of His creation" (8).

Materialism is not modern, we see. Democritus and the Epicureans who followed Heraclitus said that the *arche* was matter and empty space, with matter reduced to the *atomoi*, the fundamental particles that literally *could not be split*. The Roman poet Lucretius, attempting to spread what he regarded as the good news of the Epicurean way of life, called the atoms *semina rerum, the seeds of things*, and *primordia rerum, the first beginnings*. He did not mean that first there were atoms and then there was a universe. The atoms themselves made that interpretation impossible. There never was a time when they were not combining and recombining. Therefore, Lucretius believed that the universe had no beginning in time. Pythagoras, mathematician and mystic, said that the *arche* was number. Clearly, he did not mean that there were numbers first, and that out of those numbers burst the worlds. He meant that the foundational reality was not material but immaterial: it was not the stuff you measure, but the mathematical laws whereby you measure. It was not the instruments vibrating to the music, but the music that made them tremble. Plato found that insight most congenial and illuminating, and that is why he posted the warning above the gates to his Academy: "Let no one ignorant of geometry enter here."

For an *arche* was also a *governing principle*, the ultimate command of being, if you like. An *archaeologist* studies ancient things and their beginnings; but a *monarch* is a man who *governs alone*, as an *oligarch* is a man who *governs* with a cabal of the *few*. Forms of this Greek word are everywhere in the New Testament, and notably so in John's gospel and his letters: we have for instance the *architriklinos* or *governor of the feast* who first tastes the new wine at Cana (2:9), and the *archon* or *ruler* of this world, the Devil, whose hour to be cast out, says Jesus after he has raised Lazarus from the dead, has come (12:31).

The most stupendous instance of this word *arche*, to my mind, is found in the Apocalypse, immediately after the vision of the new heaven and the new earth, and the descent of the new Jerusalem "coming down from God out of heaven, prepared as a bride adorned for her husband" (Rev. 21:2):

> And he said unto me, It is done. I am Alpha and Omega, the beginning and the end. (21:6)

Alpha is the first letter of the Greek alphabet. Omega is the last. Does Christ here mean only to declare his position with regard to all things, that is, that he comes both at their beginning and their end, their *arche* and their *telos*? As I have said above, the Alpha and the Omega comprehend all that comes between them: to be the Alpha and the Omega is to embrace all the truth that has been spoken, that shall be spoken, and that can conceivably be spoken. The *arche*, the *beginning*, is not just the first letter of the alphabet. It is the originating fountain, ever flowing; it is the governing and fundamental reality. But all things also have an *end*. I do not mean that creatures live and die. I mean that they are made to strive for their full flourishing. The baby grows up to be a boy, who then grows to be a man, and the man in his prime marries and has children of his own. The principles of his growth and development to maturity are already present in the first seedling of life, in the zygote, in the mother's womb. To what then are all things proceeding? What is the aim of the cosmos? — for the Greek word *telos*, which we translate as *end*, suggests the motion of a javelin toward its mark. Christ says that he himself is that aim, that goal, that fulfillment. *Tetelestai*, John translates the final word of Jesus upon the cross, as he hands over his spirit to the Father: *it has been fulfilled, it is consummated* (Jn. 19:30).

So rich is that apparently simple *arche*. And then we come to *logos*, the Word. Heraclitus, who said that fire was the fundamental stuff of things, held that the *logos* informed the universe as its animating and harmonizing law, impersonal, immutable. The *logos* too was the *arche*. Did John have that sort of thing in mind? Was he speaking here the language of Greek philosophy? We need to be careful here, so as not to confuse words with thought, lest we mistake a surface similarity with a deep kinship or identity. The work that is adduced as a conduit for Greek influence, the Book of Wisdom, was surely in John's mind, but not, I think, for its being Greek in manner or matter. It is sometimes Greek in expression, but it is deeply Jewish in what it says. Its author calls upon God, the "Lord of mercy, who hast made all things with thy *word*" (Wis. 9:1, Douay-Rheims translation; Greek *logoi*). Certainly, the author of Wisdom is thinking of God who in the beginning "commanded, and they were created" (Ps. 148:5). But his imagination, or his inspiration, will not rest with that stark vision of God's creative act. Wisdom is the mediator, and though we must allow the poet his poetic license, he comes near to treating her as more than a personification, more than an allegory: "[Wisdom] reacheth therefore from end to end mightily," he says, "and ordereth all things sweetly" (Wis. 8:1). "She is a vapor of the power of God, and a certain pure emanation of the glory of the almighty God," "the brightness of eternal light and the unspotted mirror of God's majesty, and the image of his goodness" (7:25, 26). "And who shall know thy thoughts, except thou give wisdom, and send thy Holy Spirit from above?" (9:17). We are a step away from declaring what no Greek philosopher would have declared, that Wisdom is a person, with all the powers of personhood, including freedom, knowledge, love. Then may come that world-changing revelation, of Christ "the power of God, and the wisdom of God" (1 Cor. 1:24). Heraclitus had no such Wisdom or Word in mind.

Here again we must take our way with care. We walk along a narrow land bridge, with a precipice on each side. To the left is the fall into abstraction and mere philosophy. To the right is the fall into mythology and idolatry. We have here *neither Heraclitus nor Homer*, but what alone will make sense of each, and both together. So, just as we must not reduce the gospel to a footnote to Greek abstraction, so we must not to reduce the gospel to

9

a story about god-characters, Mr. and Mrs. Zeus, whether the characters are to be interpreted literally or allegorically. The gospel is not a work of man's fevered imagination, nor is it rationalism in symbolic garb. "In the beginning was the Word," says John, and if all he meant by it was old dry Stoicism sweetened with some Jewish honey, it is hard to understand why Christians would ever be persecuted by anyone. A shrug would suffice: "We are using figures of speech." Figures of speech cover a multitude of vagaries.

Likewise, we may be too accustomed to John's first verse to feel how stunning it is, as stunning as was the first chapter of Genesis, with its frank, terse, and confident rejection of everything strictly *mythological* about the creation stories of the peoples roundabout. Here we might pause to take a look at that.

"In the beginning God created the heavens and the earth"— at a stroke, the sacred author dispenses with the *theogonies* you find everywhere else, the generations of gods, such as Cronus usurping authority from his father Ouranos, and Zeus his son doing the same in turn to him, assisted by his strategic political alliance with some of the Titans, the generation of gods contemporaneous with Cronus. There is nothing of that in Genesis, or of Osiris betrayed and dismembered by his evil brother Seti, and his sister-wife Isis gathering up again all his scattered limbs; or of the Babylonian Marduk enlisting the allegiance of the younger gods to slaughter the ancient sea-goddess Tiamat, and then fashioning the universe from her remains. There is no foundational violence or conquest. There is also no star-worship, no planetary mysticism. For God made the luminaries for times and seasons, the sun to govern the day and the moon to govern the night, "and he also made the stars," says the author, as if it were an afterthought. It is a poke in the eye of the Chaldean stargazers. As a *myth* — as a story about how the moon got her spots, or why the whale is so big, the creation account in Genesis would have been a failure, but then it is not intended as a myth, that is, an explanatory story, so much as it is a stripped-down poetic revelation of what the world is: the good and wholly gratuitous creation by God, oriented toward its fulfillment in the worship of God, the feast of the Sabbath.

It is also not a piece of political propaganda. In the beginning (of the earth, that is, and of mankind), in Babylon, there was violence and empire, with Marduk emerging as the dominant god, just as the Babylonians had overrun and built upon the Sumerian civilization that came before. In the beginning (of civilization, that is), in Greece, there was political cunning and reason, in the person of Zeus, outflanking the hideous older gods of brute domination. So did the Greeks project the political organization called the *polis* back upon the conflict of the generations of the gods. In the beginning (of large-scale agriculture), in Egypt, there was a good god murdered, whose fertility and whose benevolence entered the Nile River and the mud at her banks, making Egyptian civilization possible. None of that, absolutely none of it, is to be had from our sacred author of Genesis.

One might expect the author, if we were talking simply of human agency, to present to us the holy city of Jerusalem, the "City of Peace," as present in the seed from the beginning. For man likes to cast the gods in his image, which will usually be a national or tribal image. But Jerusalem is not here. Rather the first city-builder we learn of is Cain, also the first murderer of his kin, his brother Abel. And the first prominent city in Genesis is Babel, emblem of the greatness and the folly of Babylon, and forever after the type of human confusion. Babel is the anti-word, the sign of human language itself falling into change and decay, into misunderstanding and strife.

Just as the beginning of all things is not, in Genesis, a civic myth aimed at justifying any specific place or form of human organization, so also the beginning in John is not local or specific or bound to a culture. We here are talking about all men, everywhere, and about each single man. The scope is universal, and the touch is intimate. No broader range is possible, nor any deeper gaze into the dark corners of every human soul. What cultural trappings we find are minimal, no more than is necessary for any kind of human communication to take place. We expect a people who raise corn to give us a Hiawatha, and they do. We expect a people who live beneath the steady glare of the tropical sun to give us a Quetzalcoatl, intense and merciless, demanding his daily tribute in the blood of the people's enemies. We might expect the Hebrew herdsmen to give us a god of the sheep and the cattle, but they *do not*. There was no time, and there never will come a time, when the account in Genesis of the creation and the fall of man will not speak home truths about who we are. The ancient here does not grow old. There was no time, and there never will come a time, when the opening of John's gospel will not prompt the attentive reader to ponder the very being of God, of his relationship to man and to all things, and of the inner life that is God's own, a relationship of love.

The first Christians knew, too, that what they had, the story of stories, was *not a human work* intended to explain the nature of the gods. In this regard they were at one with the Greek philosophers, who had also dismissed the stories. When, therefore, the pagans accused the Christians of unbelief, Athenagoras of Athens (c.133 – c.190) took his cue from their own philosophers. He shot back at them by showing, as the philosophers had, the incoherence of their stories, myths properly speaking. These stories say that there was a time when the gods were not. Says Athenagoras, quoting Homer, "Oceanus [was] the father of the gods and Tethys their mother" (18). But Oceanus was water, a mere material substance, and "it is unreasonable [Greek, *logos*] that matter should be older than God: for the efficient cause must necessarily precede what is created" (19).

"In the beginning was the Word." The Word: why not something else? For we might have been told something else. Why not, "In the beginning was the Power," Greek *dynamis*? Why not, "In the beginning was Will," Greek *thelema*? Muslims believe as much. Muslims tend to look upon God as sheer power, untrammeled will. When Pope Benedict XVI spoke at Regensburg in 2006, he referred to a conversation between an Islamic scholar and the Byzantine emperor Manuel Paleologos (r. 1391 – 1425), in which this very distinction was the point of debate, with the emperor saying that God does not want us to behave irrationally, literally, "without the word," because in his own will, God is never *alogos*, deprived of the word, without reason, regardless of the fact that his ways are unsearchable to us. After the works of such Aristotelian philosophers as Averroes and Avicenna were condemned as heretical, Muslim theologians have mostly rejected the notion that God creates and acts according to reason, because, in their minds, that would fetter him. They are voluntarists. God does not will a thing because it is good. God wills what he wills, and he calls good what he wills. It is conceivable that God could tomorrow command that we skulk in dark corners and kill innocent passersby, and that would be "good." Men who practiced *thugee* in the Punjab believed that the goddess Kali was pleased when they robbed and slew people on the highways. Allah does not command that, but it is not because the actions are evil in themselves.

Christians, however, in accord with the philosophers of ancient Greece, hold to the premise that evil *is no thing*, so that to imagine that God would do evil is like imagining that God could become *not God anymore*, falling into weakness and self-contradiction. For evil is not a power but a debility, as disease is not the proper condition of a body but rather its corruption, for the very "ability to sin is the ability to fail in act," says

Thomas Aquinas, and such failure "is repugnant to omnipotence."[5] If you *can* sin, you *are not almighty*. Likewise, *truth* is more than an attribute of God. For since the author and creator of the universe is *intellect*, and since the good of the intellect is *truth*, "it follows that truth is the aim of the entire universe," and that is why, says Thomas, citing Saint John, the Word was made flesh and came into the world, to "give testimony to the truth,"[6] for God is "that truth which is the prime source of all truth." He is also more than that which is supremely true, says Thomas. He is his very act of understanding: "God is his truth" (2.60). God is no more to be thought as bound by reason than as bound by goodness. Truth and goodness are not bounds laid upon God. They are his essence. They are powers.

The term *logos* had been used in various ways by Greek philosophers. For the Stoics, as I have said, it was divine and immutable but impersonal *reason* acting within the matter of the universe, animating all things according to their kinds, and binding all things together in a harmonious whole. Philo of Alexandria (d. 50 A. D.?), thinking of the Book of Wisdom and attempting to express his Jewish faith in terms that he derived from the philosophers, says that the entire universe as it is apprehended by the mind is the "idea of ideas," the very "Word of God."[7] Elsewhere he comes a little closer to attributing personhood to the Word, saying that the *logos* was the first-born of God, an intermediary between the divine and the material, as Plato's forms occupied an intermediary position between the ultimate form, that of the Good, and the formed and material creatures of the world. For "the most foundational being is God, and second is the Word of God."[8]

Many historians used to suppose that John derived his concept of the *logos* from Philo. There is no doubt that Philo exercised some influence upon early Christian interpreters of the Bible, by his method of reading the Old Testament allegorically, and by his insight that Plato could provide Christians with a conceptual language for describing their faith, and a congenial way of understanding the relationship between the immaterial and the material. Indeed, Saint Justin the Martyr, in his first *Apology* for the Christian faith he had come to embrace, argues that pagans themselves have believed in Christ the Word without understanding it so. "We have

---

5 *Summa theologiae* I, qu. 25, art. 3.
6 John 18:37; *Summa contra gentiles* I, ch. 1.
7 *On the Creation*, 6.27.
8 *Allegorical Interpretation of Genesis* 2, 3; 2.86.

been taught," he writes to the emperor Antoninus Pius, "that Christ is the first-born of God, and we have declared above that He is the Word of whom every race of men were partakers; and those who lived reasonably [that is, according to the Logos] are Christians, even though they have been thought atheists; as, among the Greeks, Socrates and Heraclitus, and men like them" (ch. 46). Antoninus was a mild-mannered man and a lover of Greek wisdom. He condemned Justin to death anyway.

But we should not stress this philosophical view of the *logos* to the exclusion of other and more powerful considerations. The Hebrews were not preoccupied with many questions that troubled the Greek mind, for example regarding the relationship of matter and form. The Hebrew faith is not thin, like a little flavored water, but thick, like blood and soup. Always in Greek philosophy, we find a trace of embarrassment that we should have bodies at all. Not nakedness so much as corporeality troubles the mind of the Greek, as it troubled the first heretics the Church had to confront, the so-called gnostics. They denied that Christ came in the flesh to redeem all flesh. But we are to rise *in the flesh*, rather than to slough off the flesh like a chrysalis and flit away into a ghostly realm of spiritual butterflies. We are to behold God "face to face" in the fullness of personality (1 Cor. 13:12), and not mind to mind, or mind to an impersonal object of the mind.

Again we might profit by searching with a Hebrew touch. Philo thought that the Greek *logos* might correspond nicely with Aramaic *memrah*, *commandment, utterance*, from the verbal root *'amar, to say*. I should like to propose a far more common noun in Scripture. The sense of Hebrew *dabar*, word, founded in the verb *dabar, to speak*, suggests a *speaking*. We really must stress the verbal power in the underlying Hebrew or Aramaic, partly hidden by the Greek *logos*, and almost buried under the Latin *verbum* and its distant cousin, the English *word*. Let me give some examples of word as act. What we call the Ten Commandments are, in Hebrew, the *ten words* of God, *'esereth ha-debarim* (Ex. 34:28 and *passim*). The word is also a *promise*, as in English: a man shall not "break his word" (Nu. 30:2). It is a *message*, as when "word came unto the king of Nineveh" (Jon. 3:6), and he repented in sackcloth and ashes. It is an *account, a story*: "My heart bursts out with a good word" (Ps. 45:2, translation mine). In the plural, it can be *deeds*: "And the rest of the acts [words] of Rehoboam, and all that he did, are they not written in the book of the chronicles [words] of the kings of Judah?" (1 Kg. 14:29). Why, to *speak a song* is to sing indeed: "Awake, awake, Deborah: awake, awake, utter a song" (Jg. 5:12).

14

When used of God, *dabar* can be a *prophetic revelation*: "The word of the Lord came expressly unto Ezekiel the priest" (Ez. 1:3). It is God's *creative power in act*: "By the word of the Lord the heavens were made; and all the host of them by the breath of his mouth" (Ps. 33:6). As the rain falls and waters the earth and brings forth life, says the Lord, "so shall my word be that goeth forth from my mouth: it shall not return to me void, but it shall accomplish that which I please" (Is. 55:11). It is thus a source of life, not in the abstract, as a wise man might give you a list of ten recommendations for living well, but in full and powerful force: "Thy word is a lamp unto my feet, and a light unto my path" (Ps. 119:105). It is before and beyond all things, because it subsists in God Himself: "The grass withereth, the flower fadeth: but the word of our God shall stand forever" (Is. 40:8).

Hence when Jesus says, in warning his disciples about the consummation of all things, "Heaven and earth shall pass away: but my words shall not pass away" (Mk. 13:31), he is claiming not merely wisdom such as a prophet might possess, or anyone who fears God, but full creative power *as the wisdom of God*. Note this well. What is implicit in the public words of Jesus that Matthew reports aroused the suspicion and enmity of those who were learned in the scriptures. The private words of Jesus that John reports leave no room for doubt. This first verse, too, leaves none.

2

And the Word was with God, and the Word was God.

HE WORD, THEN, IMPLIES MORE THAN AN IDEA, as an immaterial object of contemplation. We do not gaze upon a word. We hear it: we *heed* it. "He that hath ears to hear, let him hear," says Jesus (Mt. 11:15). It speaks to us. One of the consequences of sin is that we hear but do not heed. We shy away, as the guilty Adam did when he heard the voice of God in the garden (Gen. 3:10), or we do not hear at all, because our sins have blocked up all the passages of wisdom. "Make the heart of this people fat," says God to the prophet Isaiah, "and make their ears heavy, and shut their eyes; lest they see with their eyes, and hear with their ears, and understand with their heart, and convert, and be healed" (Is. 6:10). In Baptism, the priest touches the ear of the child and repeats the word of Jesus, when he healed the deaf man whose tongue was tied: "And looking up to heaven, he sighed, and saith unto him, Ephphatha, that is, Be opened" (Mk. 7:34). Faith comes by hearing; faith is itself a habit of hearing. "Let every man be swift to hear, slow to speak," says Saint James, so that he might "receive with meekness the engrafted *word*, which is able to save your souls" (Jas. 1:19, 21; Greek *logon*).

The Speaking of God is the foundational reality, but to whom does God speak, before he creates the world? When we speak to ourselves, it is as if we were two and not one, and often the two do not agree, so that the one Self gives the other Self orders which the other Self resists and tosses back in the teeth of the first Self. So even though each of us is but one Self, we have fallen in sin from unity to duality, "for the good that I would I do not: but the evil which I would not, that I do" (Rom. 7:19). God is the Selfsame, while we are but selves in the making — or unmaking, when we turn away from God. But to whom does God speak?

The faithful Hebrew might answer that he speaks to no one, unless it is to the beings he creates by speaking: "For he spake, and it was done" (Ps. 33:9). Let us give this suggestion its full weight. And weighty it is.

Again I must stress how radically different God's revelation to Moses and the Hebrews is from every other creation story I know of. In those stories, the gods get their hands dirty. They make things out of stuff, or they are that stuff itself in its various forms, as Apollo is not just the god of the sun, but a god that is the sun, and the nymphs are the streams they bless with their silvery dancing presence and their lustrous hair.

No such thing do we find in Genesis. The first recorded word of God is a form of his own unutterable name YHWH, in command: *yehi, be!* Be light, says God, and light came to be (Gen. 1:3). When Moses asked God from the burning bush what he was to reply when the children of Israel demanded the name of him who sent him, God says, "I AM THAT I AM" (Ex. 3:14). Names give us a handle on things; they exercise power over the things named. So was Adam granted a godlike authority over the beasts, when God brought them to him to be named, "and whatsoever Adam called every living creature, that was the name thereof" (Gen. 2:19) — remarkable submission on the part of the Lord whom the tempter is about to accuse of tyranny! But God has no such name. He cannot be circumscribed. Rather he is the circumscribing of all things, because they partake of his *being*, which he grants to them as a free gift.

But may we not go before that creation, further inward, deeper down, higher above — before, not in time, because there is no time before God makes the world of matter and time, but in being? Speaking implies relationship. Does the fullness of being not also imply relationship? The deity the Muslim worships, whom Chesterton shrewdly called "the lonely God of Omar," is a stark and gigantic monolith in the desert of existence. Commands issue forth from that Saharan deity, and sometimes mercy, but love, never, as that would suggest some need in God, and in this way the Muslim and the Greek philosopher, so tremendously different in temperament and thought, are alike. For fear of attributing to God an imperfection, the Greeks denied him a perfection, and indeed as Christians see it, the greatest perfection of all, the perfection that is love. To be is to love.

For the Word was *with* God. Our English word *with* suggests being *at the side of*: "Lo, I am with you always, even unto the end of the world," says the Lord to his disciples at Bethany (Mt. 28:20). The housemaid said of Peter, "This man was also with him" (Lk. 22:56). Or it suggests intimate *union*: "Son," says the father to the elder brother in the parable, "thou art ever with me, and all that I have is thine" (Lk. 15:31). Or even *intense opposition*: "And Jacob was left alone, and there wrestled a man with him until the breaking of the day" (Gen. 32:24; cf. English *withstand, withhold, withdraw*). None of those meanings really captures what John is saying about the Word. In none of those passages does the Greek employ the preposition that John employs.

The Word is *pros ton theon*: not merely coming forth from God, but *going toward* God. John is describing not a static condition, but a dynamism, an act. The Word is *before* God, present to him. The Baptist will say, referring to Jesus, "he was before me" — *protos mou*, in a sense that is temporal, causal, and essential: my predecessor, so to speak (Jn. 1:30). We must rule out that kind of being-before if we are talking about the Word and God. The one does not exist prior to the other. But something of *firstness* still shines in John's preposition: not that the Word is earlier than God, but that the Word *faces* God.

Faces are in more places in Scripture than the English reader will suppose. "And when Abram was ninety years old and nine, the Lord appeared to Abram, and said unto him, I am the Almighty God; walk before me, and be thou perfect" (Gen. 17:1). The Hebrew for *before* delivers a fine metaphorical sense: *hithhallek le-panai, lead thyself in the presence of my face.* The Greek translators of the Septuagint kept the metaphor alive: *enopion emou, before me* (Greek *prosopon, face*). "Thou upholdest me in mine integrity," says the psalmist to the Lord, "and settest me before thy face forever" (Ps. 41:12): *enopion sou, before thee.*

John cannot use *enopion* to describe the position of the Word before the face of God, because that echo of the Septuagint would imply that the Word was as a creature would be. But *pros* is more striking, more active, as I have suggested. "Come unto me," says Jesus, "all ye that labor and are heavy laden, and I will give you rest" (Mt. 11:28): *unto me, pros me*. The Word was face to face with God, present unto God, and how could this be?

Someone may say here that the Word is an allegory for the *wisdom of God*, herself given a face and a will in lyrical passages from Proverbs and Wisdom. When God spoke his commands to the sea and the earth, appointing their limits and foundations, then, says Wisdom, "I was by him, as one brought up with him: and I was daily his delight, rejoicing always *before him*" (Pr. 8:30): Hebrew *le-panaio*, Greek *en prosopoi autou, before his face*. And the sacred author treads very close to affirming that Wisdom is no mere allegory but a personal being, who speaks to men whom she loves: "I love them that love me, and those that seek me early shall find me" (8:17).

But John eliminates all possibility of allegory, and his rejection of the symbol is an affirmation of the real: *kai theos en ho logos*. The English translation we are accustomed to fails us here, as it softens the emphasis of John's deliberate inversion of the expected word order: *and he was GOD, the Word was!* So real it is, that Word names more than a role, such as *Redeemer*, or even a relation, such as *Son*. It is, says Saint Thomas, a *personal name*. Think of the three components of our own acts of speech. We begin with a thought, an interior intention, then we go on to express the intention in words, which are human words rather than mere sounds only because they are signs in a language. Therefore the word is most fundamentally that interior intention, that "conception of the intellect," which in the Father is not something *about* Son. It *is the Son*: and so "of all those things that pertain to the intellect, the only thing that can be predicated *personally* of the divine persons is Word, because only Word signifies that which rays forth from another."[1]

Here I wish to coin a term to describe how the *form* of John's poetry springs from the kernel, the heart, of what he is revealing to us about Christ. Think again of a monolith in the desert. It stands. It goes nowhere. The sands may blow against it, but they may as well be nothing at all. The bald bleak stone is, and that is all. It does not exist in relationship. It has no story. What truth it expresses is stark, unchanging. Or think, more dynamically, of a fountain, ever flowing-forth, but alone, and flowing because that is what it inevitably does. It does not will, it does not love. The fountain is *before* the streams that flow from it. It is their *arche*, their ground of being. We *might* say that the flowing streams are the story of the fountain, but again that seems too safely metaphorical. The streams are *from* the fountain, and in a lower pool of being the fountain is *in* the streams, because otherwise they would not exist at all. A narrative of the fountain would be a narrative of the streams, from beginning to end, at each splash expressing, in a shadowy way, the fountain from which they came.

But *the speaking* that is the Word, speaking before the face of God, and that *is God himself*, is not like the monolith or the fountain. It is like a dance of being: the *perichoresis* or *dancing-round* that the Church fathers call the inner life of the Trinity. What kind of poetry, what kind of narrative would be fittest for that dance? It would demand poetry, too, the universal human art, and the highest, the art that uses for its matter not rocks or

---

1 *Summa theologiae* I, qu. 34, art. 1.

pigments but words, thoughts. It could not be language as mere signposts, declaring facts. That is static, and it reduces the words to instruments. It could not be a language that follows the linear progression of a modern novel. That fails to capture the eternity of the Word.

I think that John has hit upon it. At first, I thought to call it *braided narrative*, with motifs winding in and about one another, advancing but always returning. But perhaps a better term would be *perichoretic narrative*: *the narrative of dancing*. We see it all through John's prologue, and in every long speech in the gospel, and in many of his third-person descriptions, and in the letters attributed to him, and, I assert, in many places in the Apocalypse. We see it, I will suggest, in the form of his gospel as a whole, full of returns and resumptions, and seeming to end but not ending yet: "A little while," says Jesus, "and ye shall not see me: and again, a little while, and ye shall see me" (Jn. 16:16). Jesus was betrayed, but that was not the end. He was crucified, but that was not the end. He rose on the third day, but that was not the end. He ascended on high, and still that was not the end. There is no end, and the end has always been, because it was in the beginning.

This braided or perichoretic narrative requires a highly peculiar sort of image-weaving and word-weaving, hardly to be found in the New Testament outside of John's gospel, his letters, and the Apocalypse.

To see what I mean, let us look at the first verse of the prologue as a whole, appending the second verse:

> In the beginning was the Word, and the Word was before God, and
> God was the Word. He was in the beginning before God.

I mean *before*, of course, as in *before the face of*, but without losing the sense of firstness. If we label the motifs by letters, what we have is this:

> In A was B, and B was before C, and C was B. [B] was in A before C.

But since God is by his very being the first, we might recast the labeling so:

> In C was B, and B was before A, and A was B. [B] was in C before A.

If you believe that that is meant to dazzle the mind, you are right. Surely the evangelist cannot possibly continue in that form, all the way through eighteen verses of the prologue? But he does. And why not? These are the deepest meditations of an old man, one who reclined at table with Jesus, who looks upon everything he saw the Lord do and heard him say, from the vantage not just of Israel and Rome, or of the story of the chosen people from Abraham to the apocalypse. He looks upon the eternal from the eternal.

Have I fallen into a trap here? I have been suggesting that we must listen to the Hebrew whispering behind the Greek that was John's second or third language. Who can compose poetry of the highest quality, unless it is in his mother tongue? But I am not making any claims here of a kind of artistic excellence proper to someone who works in a medium so familiar to him that it seems but the extension of his hand and his will. The artistic excellence in John is inextricable from *what* he is saying. My claim is not that he has found the most artfully verbal way to say it, but that he has found the only essentially *proper* way to say it. He is not fluent in Greek, as Luke is. He is not a wordsmith. He has a grasp upon a small host of words of power, and he moves those words, or those words move him, as the mystery of what they express seizes him, ever returning, recapitulating, resuming, dancing, showing forth the beginning in the end and the end in the beginning.

"And when I saw him," says John, the man who has looked upon the ages, "I fell at his feet as dead. And he laid his right hand upon me, saying unto me, 'Fear not; I am the first and the last: I am he that liveth, and was dead; and, behold, I am alive for evermore, Amen; and have the keys of hell and of death. Write the things which thou hast seen, and the things which are, and the things which shall be hereafter'" (Rev. 1:17–18). It is a choreograph of motifs: seeing, dying, first, last, living, past, present, and to come. But as in all great choreography, the movements you see in several moments of time are themselves all together a movement in a greater stretch of time. Thus the parts of the choreograph are self-similar, from the grain to the corn in ear to the field of corn to the earth as a kernel in the corn of worlds upon worlds. That is how John composes his poetry: "Except a corn of wheat fall into the ground and die, it abideth alone: but if it die, it bringeth forth much fruit" (Jn. 12:24).

I said above that this perichoretic narrative was peculiar to John. That is not quite right. There is one poet whose word-dancing did fall into the ground of John's heart and mind and soul, and there it bore fruit. That poet is the Lord:

> Judge not, that ye be not judged. For with what judgment ye judge,
> ye shall be judged: and with what measure ye mete, it shall be
> measured to you again. And why beholdest thou the mote that is

21

in thy brother's eye, but considerest not the beam that is in thine
own eye? Or how wilt thou say to thy brother, Let me pull out
the mote out of thine eye; and behold, a beam is in thine own
eye? Thou hypocrite, first cast out the beam out of thine own
eye; and then shalt thou see clearly to cast out the mote out of
thy brother's eye. (Mt. 7:1–5)

The grammar of those first two sentences might be signified so, with A
for judging, B for measuring, * for the passive, ** for the verbal noun, C
for "ye" as subject, and C# for "you" as object:

Not C A, not C A*, for A ** C A, C A*: and B** C B, B* C#.

It is not that Jesus sometimes speaks like John, but that John so longed
to speak and think like Jesus, that something of the Lord's inimitable
way took root in him. For the Lord did not so much have a way, as that
he *was the way.*

3

All things were made by him; and without him was not any thing made that was made.

Silence, ye troubled waves, and thou Deep, peace,
Said then th' Omnific Word. [1]

THIS VERSE BROACHES A NEW MOTIF, THAT OF *making*. We are meant to think again of the first words of Genesis: "In the beginning, God created the heavens and the earth" (Gen. 1:1). So the previous verses are a beginning before that beginning; and yet we must pause here, to note something important about John's choice of words. The opening to the Septuagint uses the common Greek word for making: *En arche epoiesen ho Theos ton ouranon kai ten gen.* The verb is the imperfect of *poiein, to make;* cf. English *poet,* ultimately from Greek *poeta, a maker* of songs. But the word in Hebrew is not from the common verb for making, *'asa.* It is instead the much rarer *bara,* usually rendered as *create,* and in the Old Testament this verb is predicated *only of God.* Now, there is a Greek word for *creation* in the sense of God's fashioning of things: *ktizein, to create; ktisis, creature;* and God is the *Ktistes, Creator.* John does not use that word either, though it was not a difficult one; Saint Peter, no native speaker of Greek, uses it: "Let them that suffer according to the will of God commit the keeping of their souls to him in well doing, as unto a faithful *Creator*" (1 Pt. 4:19; Greek *Ktistei*).

Perhaps John felt that that word was too earthy. He wanted a word that would imply power, but not simply power over material things. After all, God creates more than things like the stars. "A clean heart *create* in me, O God," cries the sorrowing David, convicted of the double sin of murder and adultery (Ps. 51:12); the Hebrew verb is *bara,* and the Greek in the Septuagint is a form of *ktizein.* What word would suggest

---

1   Milton, *Paradise Lost,* 7.216–17.

an intimacy deeper than that which David invokes as he begs God to make him new?

We want a verb that encompasses all things that God brings into being, including such things as cannot be seen and touched, but known only in the soul. We want to suggest by that verb not simply instances of God's action, but the whole sweep of it from first to last, from the alpha to the omega. And we want somehow to associate that verb closely with Christ. What John chooses is what a child might choose: the verb *genesthai, to become, to be, to happen, to be born, to be begotten.* The verb is everywhere in the New Testament: it is there whenever the good translator says, "And it *came to pass," kai egeneto.* By a fine coincidence, the Hebrew *bara* can be extended to include *birth*: "I will judge thee in the place where thou *wast created,* in the land of thy nativity," says the Lord to the Ammonites (Ez. 21:35; Hebrew *nibre'eth*).

How might we render John's words, then, to illuminate the sheer comprehensive power he attributes to the Word? By him, all things came to pass (*egeneto*), and nothing that came to pass (*egeneto*) did so without him. All things happened through him, and no happening came to happen without him. All things were begotten through him, and without him nothing was begotten, that was begotten. That last rendering is the most suggestive, because it will resound when John raises the verb to an inconceivable height: for Christ is the *monogenos, the only-begotten.* John is not alone in this exalted Christology. So too that brilliant artist of Scriptural interpretation, the author of the letter to the Hebrews, in affirming that Christ is "the brightness of [God's] glory, and the express image of his person, and upholding all things through the word [*rhema,* not *logos*] of his power," says that he was "made [*genomenos*] so much better than the angels," for "unto which of the angels said he at any time, Thou art my son, this day have I begotten [*gegenneka*] thee?" (Heb. 1:3–5, citing Ps. 2:7).

What does the evangelist mean, however, when he says that all things came to pass *through* the Word? The King James translation, almost always sensitive to figurative meanings and suggestions made present in and through the literal, here is a bit weak: "All things were made by him." John's preposition, *dia,* is the strongest possible for what he wants to express. It means *through,* suggesting motion all the way through to the end. It is not the most common word for mere instrumentality or agency. So God "spake by [*dia*] the mouth of his holy prophets, which have been since the world began," says Zacharias the father of the Baptist

(Lk. 1:70). The prophet is not some inanimate trumpet to be played and then set aside. He is fully himself and fully energized by the Lord; most fully himself, because most filled with God. Or, for a terrible alternative, even a sinner may be wholly taken up in God's providential plan. "Truly the Son of man goeth," says Jesus to his apostles at the Last Supper, "but woe unto that man by [*dia*] whom he is betrayed!" (Lk. 22:22).

So Milton in *Paradise Lost* describes the Son as bearing in himself the fullness of the Father's creative power:

> And thou my Word, begotten Son, by thee
> This I perform, speak thou, and be it done. (7.163 – 64)

> So spake th' Almighty, and to what he spake
> His Word, the Filial Godhead, gave effect. (7.174 – 75)

> Heav'n opened wide
> Her ever-during Gates, Harmonious sound
> On golden Hinges moving, to let forth
> The King of Glory in his powerful Word
> And Spirit coming to create new worlds. (7.205 – 9)

Many critics say, with some justification, that Milton was an Arian heretic, believing that Christ was the first *creation* of the Father, made by the Father co-equal to himself. Be that as it may, the Word of God he portrays in action here in creating world upon world is much closer to the Word as revealed to us in the words of Saint John than he is to a mere teacher, or to any man we might appreciate and patronize. Let us never reduce Christ to mere greatness.

To say that all things were made, or come to pass, or are begotten not merely by but *through* the Word, the Speaking, is to rule out any opposition between Creator and Redeemer. We must never speak glibly and disparagingly about the "God of the Old Testament." We must not revive the heresy of Marcion (fl. 140 – 160), who demoted God the Creator to a "demiurge," not evil but also not supremely good. Marcion therefore rejected the Old Testament as all too fleshly and bloody for sophisticated Hellenes, and he riddled the New Testament with holes to boot. We may say, warily, that the children of Israel dwelt in twilight, and that their knowledge of the great I AM dawned upon them slowly, as God revealed to them, step by step, light upon light, what they were ready to understand, though when we look back upon that revelation we see its maturity and fullness always already present in the seed.

25

God is *always* the God of mercy and love, which flow from his very being. The just Father is loving, and the loving Son is just. Cries the psalmist in triumph: "O give thanks unto the Lord; for he is good: because his mercy endureth for ever" (Ps. 118:1). The Hebrew for that verse is monumental. What we in English must express as a whole clause, "for he is good," in Hebrew is only two words, *ki tob* — for [*he is*] *good*; and the Hebrew who sang those would hear the echo of their first use in Scripture: "And God saw the light, *that it was good*" (Gen. 1:3, my translation; Hebrew *ki tob*). The goodness of light and of all creatures derives from the essential goodness of God. And any notion that Christ is a flower child who gives people the comfort they wish and not the justice they will by their deeds cannot be squared with the plain words of the man himself, who "shall separate them one from another, as a shepherd divideth the sheep from the goats" (Mt. 25:32).

There is no distinction between creation as the prophets and the evangelists understood it, and governance. It is not as if God the Father makes a universal machine and then gives it to the Son to administer. The very stones will cry out if we do not heed the words of Christ himself. "These things saith the Amen, the faithful and true witness, the beginning [*arche*] of the creation of God," says Christ the ruler of all things to the tepid church at Laodicea (Rev. 3:14). That Amen, so beloved of the evangelist John that he remembers Jesus as uttering it all the time, expresses more than a wish. It bears the full weight of glory and truth, and truth as trustworthiness, fidelity, strength. "He who blesses himself in the earth," says Isaiah in the throes of prophetic joy, "shall bless himself in the God of Amen," for "behold, I shall create new heavens, and a new earth" (Is. 65:16 – 17; translation mine). "Behold," says God upon the throne, as the heavenly Jerusalem descends, "I make all things new" (Rev. 21:5).

Why did John say that "without him was not any thing made that was made," when he has already said that "all things were made by him"? Is that not redundant? Let me venture two suggestions here.

The first is that, again, John is thinking in his native tongue. He likes things in pairs, and so do Hebrew poets. We in English like to make verbs out of nouns: as if the objects are first, and what they do comes second. The Hebrews liked to make nouns out of verbs: as if actions are first, and the things that act make themselves manifest as such. A noun next to its participle or verb will often make for a fine and memorable pair, as when God gives man dominion over "every *creeping thing that creepeth*" upon the earth (Gen. 1:26). The Hebrew is *ha-remesh ha-romesh* — *creeper creeping*, as we might jauntily say. Or when God warns Adam and Eve against eating of the fruit of the tree of the knowledge of good and evil, he says that on the day they eat of it they shall "die the death" (Gen. 2:17; translation mine); the Hebrew is *moth tamuth*. So I suspect that in John's mind, the verb "make" shone out as verb and participial noun, together.

Another kind of pair that Hebrew poets were fond of was the positive and negative way of saying the same thing, on either side of a verse:

> For the Lord knoweth the way of the righteous:
> but the way of the ungodly shall perish. (Ps. 1:6)

> But thou art the same,
> and thy years shall have no end. (Ps. 102:27)

> He should still live for ever,
> and not see corruption. (Ps. 49:9)

Why should John give us such a pair here? In logic, it is the same to say that through Christ all things were made, and that *without* him — Greek *choris*, literally *apart from, sundered from* — nothing was made. In the heart it is not so. It is one thing to consider that all things are filled with the creative power of the Word, and that "the invisible things of him from the creation of the world are clearly seen, being understood by the things that are made, even his eternal power and Godhead" (Rom. 1:20). It is another to consider that outside of that power there is nothing, vanity, emptiness, unmeaning. To turn from Christ is not to turn toward something else. It is to turn toward uncreation. So, says Saint Paul, the pagans "became vain in their imaginations, and their foolish heart was darkened" (Rom. 1:21), and, failing to worship God as God, they ended up casting him in the image of man, then birds, and beasts, and creeping things, and so too were they darkened in their desires, "for even their women did change the natural use into that which is against nature: and likewise also the men, leaving the natural use of the woman, burned in their lust one toward another" (1:26–27). It is also to turn toward futility. "I am the vine, ye are the branches," says Christ, as John reports. "He that abideth in me, and I in him, the same bringeth forth much fruit: for without [*choris*] me ye can do nothing" (Jn. 15:5). You might as well put yourself out of the world.

4

In him was life ...

Approach ye then with faithful hearts sincere,
And take the safeguard of salvation here.
He that in this world rules his saints and shields,
To all believers life eternal yields:
With heavenly Bread makes them that hunger whole,
Gives living waters to the thirsty soul.
Alpha and Omega, to whom shall bow
All nations at the Doom, is with us now. [1]

JOHN DOES NOT SAY, "LIFE WAS IN HIM," OR "HE
was alive." The sense of the previous verse carries over to this one.
Life was in the Word essentially, and without the Word there is no
life. In *him* was life, and nowhere else. "I am the way, the truth, and the
life," says Jesus (Jn. 14:6). "I am the resurrection and the life" (Jn. 11:25).
"The water I shall give him," says Jesus to the woman at the well, "shall
be in him a well of water springing up into everlasting life" (Jn. 4:14).
"I am the bread of life," he says, and in his Aramaic it would have been
a fine and sonorous phrase indeed: *'ani lehem le-chayim*, with *lehem*, bread,
meaning by amplification *feast* (cf. Dan. 5:1), as if Jesus had meant, "I am
the feast of life." "To whom shall we go?" says Simon Peter, when many
of the disciples left Jesus, not understanding what he said about his flesh
and blood. "Thou hast the words of eternal life" (Jn. 6:68).

I will pause here to comment upon what Peter has said, as John remembers. If we "translate" it into the sacred language that Peter and the other
apostles heard and sang, he has said something like this: *With-thee [the-words
life-unto-everlasting]*. Hebrew is notably sparing of prepositions and verbal
operators whose function it is to relate one word with another. There is
no "of," here, and what I have rendered by "with" and "unto" is in each
case but a single consonant. What we hear otherwise is *thee the-words life*

---

1   "Draw Near and Take the Body of the Lord," Latin, 7th c., *Sancti, venite, Christi
Corpus sumite*, trans. John Mason Neale.

everlasting. The final word is most powerful, resounding in the highest and most joyful praises that the Jews rendered to God. Again the psalmist: "O give thanks unto the Lord; for he is good: because his mercy endureth for ever" (Ps. 118:1). In Hebrew that last clause is but three words: *ki le-'olam chasdo*. Peter has attributed to Christ's words the characteristic that the psalmist attributes to the mercy of God: they are of life *le-'olam*. And if we recall that for the Hebrew, *words* can denote not only verbal things, ringing in the ear, but promises and deeds, we can see that Peter's confession here is parallel to his outburst of faith — of trust in the everlasting rock of truth, recorded by the other evangelists: "Thou art the Christ, the Son of the living God" (Mt. 16:18).

Again, we are not talking about a mere figure of speech. Jesus is not Buddha. He does not merely give life, of a sort. He *is* life, pure and perfect. So John sees in a vision "a pure river of water of life, clear as crystal, proceeding out of the throne of God and of the Lamb" (Rev. 22:1), like the blood and water which the soldier set abroach when he pierced the side of Christ upon the cross (Jn. 19:34).

Saint Paul says the same, in many of the same words, though in his own style. If we are risen with Christ, we are to set out hearts on things above, for "ye are dead, and your life is hid with Christ in God," with Christ, "who is our life" (Col. 3:3 – 4). But what is that life? What does it mean, to be alive?

The Greek had at least two nouns for life. One was *bios*. If you wanted to record the course of someone's life, his words and deeds, his being born in Neapolis and his dying in Sousa, you would write his *bios* (cf. English *biography*). If you wanted on stage to portray someone "to the life," as we used to say, you must become a *biologos* (cf. English *biology*, the science of living things as opposed to the inanimate). "It's a living," says the coal miner with a shrug, not meaning that he loves it, but that by it he manages to keep a roof over his family's heads. That would be *bios*, as when the father in the parable divided among his two sons "his living" (Lk. 15:12).

It occurs to me that when modern man thinks of life, he thinks of *bios*: the food and drink and raiment that Jesus says we are not to worry about, the means for keeping alive, the course of a career, and so forth. So when modern man imagines the kingdom of God, insofar as he can imagine it at all, he reduces it to *bios*, as do the Muslims in their paradise that is an oasis with a harem of beautiful women, and plenty of sweet fruit and drink. So did the humble Indian, says Alexander Pope, imagine in his simple humility a heaven that would be like the home he had before the Christian colonists came thirsting for gold:

> To be, contents his natural desire,
> He asks no angel's wing, no seraph's fire;
> But thinks, admitted to that equal sky,
> His faithful dog shall bear him company. [2]

One of the odd things about the word *bios* — and certainly no one in John's time knew this — is that it is related to words that do not appear to resemble it at all, nor do the words resemble one another: English *quick* and Latin *vivus*, for example. It is also related to the Greek *zoe*, from which we derive words having to do with living animals: *protozoa, zoology*. But in the New Testament, *zoe* is a powerful word, quite distinct from *bios*. Think of the moment in Genesis, when God formed Adam from the dust and "breathed into his nostrils the *breath of life*; and man became *a living soul*" (Gen. 2:7). The Greek of the Septuagint is *pnoen zoes*; the Hebrew is *nishmoth chayim*. Adam, with the name-punning the Hebrews were so fond of, calls his wife Eve, *Chawwah*, because she is to be mother of all *chai*: all man alive. "See, I have set before thee this day," says the aged Moses to the assembled people, "life and good, and death and evil" (Dt. 30:15). That is *zoe* in the Septuagint Greek, and *chayim* in Hebrew.

What does the word mean? If we are talking about *bios*, unless someone is in the grip of a terminal illness, we admit of no degrees. George is no more or less alive than is Henry, so long as they both are breathing and walking about. Imagine that they are shopping in the mall. George is there to buy his wife a great spray of roses for her birthday, and is thinking of their seven children happily hunting for presents here and there to give to their mother, and how their faces will beam with delight when she opens them. George is alive, as Saint Irenaeus had in mind when he said that the glory of God is man alive: *Gloria Dei est vivens homo*. But Henry is alone and aimless. He has no one to give to, and no one to give him a gift. He has perhaps fallen for a modern form of the old lie, that man is his own to dispense with as he pleases, so he wanders toward a book shop, not for any wisdom to be found therein, but for a pornographic magazine. He is *dispirited*, and it shows in his eyes. *Superbia diaboli est moriens homo*, we might say: the devil's pride is a man dying inside.

Eternal life is not perpetual breathing. It is the life of life: the life whereof a good man's joy is but a shadow, or an anticipation. It is made

---

2 · *Essay on Man*, I.109–12.

available to us in Christ, and in Him alone. How should we expect otherwise? The living God speaks the Word that is coeternal with himself, the
Word through whom all things are made. If we want life, we must go to
the Word. We must become *alive in the living Word.*

If we understand the full implications of that declaration, *In him was
life,* we will understand also why Jesus says that unless we eat the flesh of
the Son of man and drink his blood, we shall have within us no life (Jn.
6:53): *bios* is not denied but is taken up into *zoe.* The teaching scandalizes
rationalists today as it scandalized the learned of Jesus's own time. So Leo
Tolstoy, in his final novel *Resurrection,* describes an Orthodox service with
satirical gusto, the satire more powerful for its narrowness of vision and
the great man's deliberate refusal even to try to understand what Christians
have thought about the sacrament of life, from the very first:

> After having asked the children their names the priest carefully
> took a bit of bread soaked in wine out of the cup with a spoon
> and thrust it far into the mouth of each child in turn, while the
> subdeacon, wiping the children's mouths, in a gay voice sang a
> song about the children's eating God's flesh and drinking His
> blood. After that the priest carried the cup behind the partition,
> and drinking up all the blood left in the cup and eating all the
> remaining bits of God's body, and painstakingly licking round his
> moustaches and wiping his mouth and the cup, briskly marched
> out from behind the partition, in the most cheerful frame of mind,
> the thin soles of his calfskin boots creaking slightly as he walked. [3]

Very well done, that, but wrong. Tolstoy might have heeded the words
of Ignatius of Antioch, writing to the church at Rome, and warning them
before he arrives that they should not discourage him from the martyrdom for which he longs. "I have no relish for corruptible food, or for the
sweet things of this life. The bread of God is what I want, which is the
flesh of Christ, of the seed of David, and for drink I want his blood — a
deathless feast of love" (7:3). The same Ignatius urges us to share the one
bread of the Eucharist, which is the "*medicine* of immortality" — Greek
pharmakon, as of a healing drug (cf. English *pharmacy*) — and, literally,
the antidote, the remedy whereby we shall not die but have life in Christ
forever. [4] One thing about drugs and antidotes: you do have to consume
them. For Christ came not in an idea, but in the flesh.

---

3 From Part One, ch. 39.
4 *Smyrn.* 20:2.

... and the life was the light of men.

O Splendor of God's glory bright,
O thou that bringest light from light,
O Light of Light, light's living spring,
O Day, all days illumining! [5]

HERE JOHN TURNS TO THE FIRST WORDS OF Genesis again, and to its most glorious motif: *light*. No mere man can exhaust its significance. The sacred author bound the light to the very being of God, in words that suggest that nothing could be nearer to Him. The Hebrew breaks upon us in glorious simplicity: *Wayyomer Elohim*, "*Yehi 'or*," *wa yehi 'or*. As we might put it in blocks of English, "And said God, 'Be light,' and be light." The author has played upon a peculiarity of Hebrew, whereby the verb form for the past tense, when it follows the conjunction *and* (Hebrew *wa*), is identical to the verb form for the subjunctive used in a future sense. So what in English are two very different verbal phrases, "let there be" and "there was," are in this Hebrew construction the same: *yehi*. There was no finer way for the author to suggest the instantaneous and unmediated nature of God's creation. The light's existence is inseparable from God's speech. And the verb itself, *be*, is a play on the very name of God: I AM, abbreviated in Hebrew names as *Yah* or *Yo*: *Joab* = *Yoab*, *God is Father*. God whose essence it is to exist, as Thomas Aquinas aptly puts it, imparts existence to the light, *and so it was*. No other act of creation in Genesis is described with this verbal instantaneity.

What is this light? If we say we know for certain, we lie, and the truth is not in us, as John himself might say (cf. 1 Jn. 1:8). We can be certain that it is not the light of sun and moon and stars, which have yet to be made. Perhaps it is the light of intellect. Perhaps it is the prime energy of all created things, to be shared out among them. For many of the Church Fathers, above all St. Augustine, this "light" was the angelic realm. The great Milton, so habitually sure in his mind about all things in Scripture, is not sure here:

Hail holy Light, offspring of Heav'n first-born,
Or of th' Eternal Coeternal beam
May I express thee unblamed? Since God is Light,

---

5   St. Ambrose (340–397), *Splendor paternae gloriae*, tr. Robert Bridges, 1899.

> And never but in unapproached Light
> Dwelt from Eternity, dwelt then in thee,
> Bright effluence of bright essence increate.[6]

For "God is light," says John (1 Jn. 1:5), and the "Father of lights," says James (Jas. 1:17), and the heavenly Jerusalem needs neither sun nor moon, for the Lamb "is the light thereof" (Rev. 21:23).

This light, the light whence all things derive their light, is the "light of men." The translators of the New American Bible, who do not understand poetry, render the phrase as "light of the human race." They do so because they are allergic to the generic masculine term *man*, thinking that it is an offense to women. Their translation is wrong on several counts. First, there were ways in Greek to express the general concept of the human race. John does not employ them, and whether he knew of them or not, we translate what he did say, not what we wish he had said. Second, the *human race* is a collective term, tending to abstraction: from our experience of a variety of human beings, we abstract the idea of the race. But John is not talking about an idea. Third, *the human race* does not mean the same thing as *men*, because it does not capture the concrete, singular, personal *man*. I can think about the human race all day long, and never once see in my mind any distinct *man* or *men*, any Peter, James, or John. But I must think of a distinct man if I am to think of Christ. He came not to save a collective or an abstraction or a quality. He came to save Peter, James, and John; and Mary of Bethany, and Martha, and the children who gathered around him. Theologians call it the "scandal of particularity," and it is bound up with the Incarnation itself: imagine, as C. S. Lewis says, that the redemptive plan of God should "[sharpen] at last into one small bright point like the head of a spear," namely "a Jewish girl at her prayers." In Christ and in Christ alone is each member of the body fully a man and Christ. So our translations should respect the words in their exactitude, and should give us man both singular and universal. My modern French translation does so: the life was *la lumiere des hommes*. My modern Italian translation does so: the life was *la luce degli uomini*. Why should we be afraid of the word?

I have said that no creation in Genesis is like the creation of light, for its immediacy and its poetic and verbal intimacy with the very name and being of God. Light is the originating fountain for the creatures that follow. But there is a creature who does more than thrive in the light, as plants and

---

6 *Paradise Lost*, 3.1–6.

animals do. It is the creature that consummates all the physical creation that came before: it is *man*. Again, we are not talking about a collective. Every individual man is that consummation, that pinnacle; each one, and all together. The sacred author did not have God say, "Let there be man, and there was man." He says something even more powerful, and endlessly mysterious. "Let us make man in our image, after our likeness," says God (Gen. 1:26). That cannot be understood in man-shaped terms. After all, to make "any graven image, or any likeness" of things in the world, to stand in as symbols of the deity, is akin to worshiping a false god in place of the true one (Ex. 20:3 – 4). Everywhere else in the world, man happily indulges his mythopoeic imagination, and pictures his gods, even if they are but hideous monoliths on a sacred island, or earth goddesses with immense buttocks, fit for fertility. Everywhere but in Israel, where the first revelation about man is that he is made in the image and likeness of God.

Here it may help to turn to the Greek of the Septuagint. The word for *image* is *eikon*, from which we derive English *icon*. An *eikon* is literally something you look at, as we see in Byzantine sacred art, whereby the artist deep in prayer and submitting to tradition effaces himself in order to render most powerfully the truth in visual form. The word for *likeness* is *homoiosis*, that is, the state of being *homoios* or *similar* to something or someone. Here we must take care to notice that similarity in appearance can have a direction. We say of a portrait of Washington that it is a *likeness* of the man. But the man is not a likeness of the portrait. The gift of likeness in this case travels in one direction. We say of a little boy playing in the sandbox that he looks like his father at the construction site. We do not say that the father looks like his little son playing in the sandbox. Man is like God, but God is not like man: "To whom then will ye liken me, or shall I be equal? saith the Holy One" (Is. 40:25), in contempt for the foolishness of idolatry. The Greek gods in the epics of Homer behave like human beings, and often indecent human beings at that, but God, calling upon his people to forsake their all too human sins, says, "My thoughts are not your thoughts, neither are your ways my ways" (Is. 55:8). "Thou savorest not the things that be of God," says Jesus to Peter, rebuking him for his perfectly human wish to keep Jesus safe from his enemies, "but those that be of men" (Mt. 16:23). The name of the prince of the angels asks the right rhetorical question: Michael, *Who is like God?* No one and nothing, if we consider God in his essence and his greatness. No one looks like God. And yet the same God has in fact made man in his likeness.

34

The first created light, which is not the light of sun or moon, is thus to be considered alongside man the final-created, who bears God's image and likeness, not because God is like him, but because in a mysterious way he is like God. Each one singly, each person you meet, is an unrepeatable instantiation of the image of God. But man, *ha 'adam*, is also *mankind*, made for love of God and of one another. The image of the three-personed God is in each man singly and in man universally, for man is a social being. Hence the two great commandments imply one another. Says Jesus:

> The first of all the commandments is, Hear, O Israel: The Lord our God is one Lord:
> And thou shalt love the Lord thy God with all thy heart, and with all thy soul, and with all thy mind, and with all thy strength: this is the first commandment.
> And the second is like, namely this, Thou shalt love thy neighbor as thyself. (Mk. 12:29–31)

What does it mean that the life was "the light of men"? John joins the author of Job, and the psalmists, and Isaiah (whether there was one or two authors for the book of Isaiah in this respect makes no difference, since the motif of light is all throughout it), and Saint Paul as poets of light. Job longs for the time when God showered his favor upon him, "when his candle shined upon my head, and when by his light I walked through darkness" (Job 29:3). For the psalmist, the word of God is "a lamp unto my feet, and a light unto my path" (Ps. 119:105). "The people that walked in darkness," says Isaiah, in the throes of messianic vision, "have seen a great light" (Is. 9:2); and there will come a time beyond sun and moon, when "the Lord shall be unto thee an everlasting light, and thy God thy glory" (Is. 60:19). Saint Paul urges us to "put on the armor of light" (Rom. 13:12), and to "walk as children of light" (Eph. 5:8). He who loves his brother, says John, "abideth in the light" (1 Jn. 2:10).

As always, I urge the reader not to reduce this light to a metaphor. It is at least a metaphor, of course, because it is meant to carry across a meaning or meanings that do not inhere in the literal word. When Jesus says that his disciples are to be "the light of the world," he is not talking about incandescence, but about the shining-forth of their deeds (Mt. 5:14). But that same shining-forth in other scriptural verses expresses the being of God, the light of his countenance — a countenance that the children of Israel were not permitted to imagine, to engrave it in stone and thereby make it like the countenance of a man, or, worse, like the face of a beast or a monster of human idolatry. It is not merely good will that the psalmist begs for, when he prays, "Lord, lift thou up the light of thy countenance upon us" (Ps. 4:6). Think of the light of a face breaking into a smile; that is a mere shadow of the light that the psalmist, pushing against the limits of human language, longs to see.

Light is not only the object of our vision. Light is not passive, possessing the bare minimum of existence. It is active, powerful, flourishing in existence and intellect. It is the way of vision: it is what enables us to see at all: "For with thee is the fountain of life: in thy light shall we see light" (Ps. 36:9). When Jesus healed the man born blind, and his world was filled with light, the leaders of the Jews tried to persuade the fellow that Jesus was but a sinner. The healed man saw more than they did. He saw that his healing was like a new creation: "Since the world began was it not heard that any man opened the eyes of one that was born blind" (Jn. 9:32). "I am the light of the world," says Jesus (9:5).

5

And the light shineth in the darkness; and the darkness comprehendeth it not.

LMOST ALL TRANSLATIONS NOW READ "HAS not overcome" for the Greek *ou katelaben*. It is an acceptable translation. But it does not capture the force of John's word, as I will show. When Jesus says, after he has warned his apostles of troubles to come, "Be of good cheer; I have overcome the world" (Jn. 16:33), John uses for his expression the verb for winning a victory, *nikein*. He did not need to take Greek in with his mother's milk to find that word. It was common enough. The Greeks even worshiped the goddess of victory, Nike. John uses forms of that word in seven other places, in his letters: "For whatsoever is born of God overcometh the world" (1 Jn. 5:4; *nikai*). He—and the author himself says that it is he, and no other—uses its forms thirteen times in the Apocalypse: "These shall make war with the Lamb, and the Lamb shall overcome them" (Rev. 17:14; *nikesei*). That makes 21; in all the rest of the New Testament I find it ten times, most powerfully in Paul's ringing cry of triumph: "Then shall be brought to pass the saying that is written, Death is swallowed up in victory" (1 Cor. 15:54; cf. Is. 25:8).

John does mean that the darkness has not overcome the light, but he means more than that, and he intends the not-overcoming to be conceived of in a special way. The King James translators, taking their cue from Saint Jerome's Latin, *non comprehendit*, wanted to impart that special sense. What was it? The root of *katelaben* is the common verb *lambanein, to grab hold of, catch, grasp, seize.* Imagine the darkness as a primal beast, attempting to steal silently upon the light and catch it, so that it can move neither forward nor backward. It would grasp the light on both ends. It would be both before and after the light; the light would have its time to be, but the darkness would last forever. No dance of light, then. Think of the nobly sad mythology of the Norsemen, who believed that the gods of Valhalla and the giants, the forces of darkness, would fight a final battle at Ragnarok, and that the gods would lose, and the world would return to its original night. Well does such a myth fit for the lands of the long dark winter. Or think of the ancient materialist story, revived in our time, which has the universe burst into being spontaneously, but winding down over the billions of years, till all shall be swallowed up in black holes, or perhaps all shall be thinned out in a universal heat-death. Nor let us dismiss the artistic power of this terrible and tragic vision. As always, C. S. Lewis, who was temperamentally attracted to it, puts it better than any atheist has ever done. Human progress continues, he says, but

> all this time, unceasingly, out of all reach of human power, Nature, the old enemy, has been steadily gnawing away. The sun will cool — all suns will cool — the whole universe will run down. Life (every form of life) will be banished, without hope of return, from every inch of infinite space. All ends in nothingness, and "universal darkness covers all." The pattern of the myth thus becomes one of the noblest we can imagine. [1]

We can call it the *Mundane Tragedy*. But it has one most important disadvantage, if it is applied beyond the sphere of an individual figure like Macbeth, spiraling into wickedness and unbeing. Applied beyond, it happens not to be true. The words of John affirm the primacy and the eternity of life and light.

The annotators for the Catholic lectionary acknowledge, grudgingly, that *comprehend* is an alternative translation for *overcome*, but they refer us to another verse in John, a verse which for them settles the matter. It does not. Note well: scholars are not to be trusted when they trim, flatten, or brush aside, for it is always more comfortable to make less of a great thing than *to make less of yourself*. Be suspicious whenever a scholar appears to set himself and his learning higher than the thing he is teaching about. Here, the annotators have chosen the easier and less interesting of two readings, one that trims and brushes aside. For they could have referred us to an important verse in Ephesians, which might settle the matter *the other way*. These are the only other places in the New Testament where a form of *katalambanein* appears. Even if we look at the verse in John to which the annotators refer us, we see dramatic action that has to do with

---

1   From "Is Theology Poetry?," in *The Weight of Glory*.

time in its comprehensive sweep: with what we should expect as we go forth in time toward eternity. When Jesus says that he must be lifted up from the earth, to draw all men to him, the people furrow their brows and say, "We have heard out of the law that Christ abideth forever," so what can it mean that "the Son of man must be lifted up?" Jesus replies: "Yet a little while is the light with you. Walk while ye have the light, lest darkness come upon you: for he that walketh in darkness knoweth not whither he goeth. While ye have light, believe in the light, that ye may be the children of light" (12:34–36). If we do not believe in the light, the darkness may, when we least expect it, *come upon us* (*katalabei*), getting ahead of us, as it were, and cutting us off from the life to come. We will be ambushed while we foolishly waste our time. Even here, then, the sense is more than to *overcome*. It is to seize unawares. Imagine walking in the path of destruction, and not knowing where you are going, when suddenly the darkness, like a cunning and watchful beast, leaps for its prey.

But the word can be used for glory, too, as Saint Paul shows us. Paul prays for the Ephesians, that "Christ may dwell in your hearts by faith; that ye, being rooted and grounded in love, may be able to *comprehend* with all the saints what is the breadth, and length, and depth, and height; and to know the love of Christ, which passeth knowledge, that ye might be filled with all the fullness of God" (Eph. 3:17–19; *katalabesthai*). Again we tremble at the brink of a great mystery. To be filled with the fullness of God is to enjoy a blessedness so great, says Paul, we can with the saints fathom the breadth and length and depth and height of love. This too is not mere abstract understanding, but a vision of love in act, from the first moment of creation to the consummation of all things, when God shall be all in all (1 Cor. 15:28).

The light *shineth* in the darkness. We are not here talking about the shining of a lamp, for which the evangelists use quite another word. Even the face of the transfigured Christ did not shine as John says that the light shines here. Do not think of glowing or gleaming or blazing. Think instead of the very essence of light. If John had Hebrew in his mind, he would have had another wonderful noun-verb twin, the noun *light* paired with the verb it builds, to *shine with light*: as we might say *the light lightens*. But how to put that in Greek? He chooses a verb that alliterates with the word for *light*: *to phos phainei*. Both the noun and the verb are quite common. But *phainein* means more than to give off light. It means to *make manifest, to appear*. John is fond of that word and its near kin, which we find in his

39

gospel, his letters, and the Apocalypse, 24 times by my count, and only 34 times in all the other books of the New Testament put together.

It is a powerful word. "When he *shall appear*," says John, referring to the consummating manifestation of Christ at the end of time, "we shall be like him; for we shall see him as he is" (1 Jn. 3:2; *phanerothei*). "In this *was manifest* the love of God to us," says John, that he sent his only-begotten Son into the world, that the world might be saved (1 Jn. 4:9; *ephanerothei*). "After these things," he says, recalling the tremendous appearances of the risen Lord, "he *shewed* himself again to the disciples at the sea of Tiberias" (Jn. 21:1; *ephanerosen*). Again, we find that verse in the Apocalypse where the light of the Lamb is the very essence of heaven: "And the city had no need of the sun, neither of the moon, *to shine* in it: for the glory of God did lighten it, and the Lamb is the light thereof" (Rev. 21:23; *phainosin*). "For the life *was manifested*, and we have seen it, and bear witness, and shew unto you that eternal life," says John, in that prologue to his great letter which is so similar to the prologue of his gospel and to the prologue of the Apocalypse, "which was with the Father, and *was manifested* unto us" (1 Jn. 1:2; *ephanerothe*).

We must think, then, not of a candle in the night, but of an all-conquering *manifestation*, or, to use a word we are familiar with in another context, an *epiphany*. Thus the light made itself manifest in the darkness. We are at the scene of a cosmic conflict between being and un-being, between light as the very life of God, and darkness as all that in denying God tends toward the total loss of significance and existence.

Light and darkness are more than symbols for John. They mark the fundamental orientations of man. The Essenes, radical followers of the Law who lived in communities in the desert and with whom some scholars have said the Baptist associated, wrote of light and darkness all the time. We have, though, no evidence of such an association at all, and there are features of the life of the Essenes that put them worlds apart from the Baptist and Jesus; they did not permit themselves even to answer the call of nature during the Sabbath, whereas Jesus permitted his disciples on the Sabbath day to pluck ears of corn to eat, earning them the disapproval of the Pharisees (Mt. 12:1–2). The Essenes were radical separatists, while the Baptist deigns to preach to soldiers in the Roman army and counsel them (Lk. 3:14).

We need not seek out the Essenes for that contrast of light with darkness that is universal to human culture and experience. We remember

Genesis, when God divided the light from the darkness, and he called the light "day," and the darkness he called "night" (Gen. 1:5). We also recall the groanings of Job, afflicted by God and not seeing why, wishing that the very creation itself were reversed: "Let that day be darkness," he says, referring to the day of his birth, "neither let the light shine upon it" (Job 3:4). "Woe unto them," cries the prophet, "that call evil good and good evil; that put darkness for light, and light for darkness" (Is. 5:20). That is ultimately what the turn toward evil is: a turn toward universal night. So says the Light of the world: "And this is the condemnation, that light is come into the world, and men loved darkness rather than light, because their deeds were evil" (Jn. 3:19).

The poets of our Christian heritage understood the matter well. When Satan lifts his defeated angelic bones from the floor of Hell, his eyes behold

> The dismal Situation waste and wild:
> A Dungeon horrible, on all sides round
> As one great Furnace flamed, yet from those flames
> No light, but rather darkness visible
> Served only to discover sights of woe.[2]

But when Adam and Eve, thinking to grasp enlightenment on their own, eat of the fruit of the forbidden tree, and seal their guilt with lovemaking in the open field, they awake to a sad reality:

> Up they rose
> As from unrest, and each the other viewing,
> Soon found their Eyes how opened, and their minds
> How darkened. (9.1051–54)

So Dante imagines going down into the jaws of Hell, as entering a world below the earth, where sun and moon and stars never shine, day never comes, but only a little glooming light is reflected upon the existences of the damned, from Him whose nature it is to be:

> There sighs and moans and utter wailing swept
>   resounding through the dark and starless air.
> I heard them for the first time, and I wept.[3]

In *The Silmarillion*, J. R. R. Tolkien's evil spider Ungoliant devours light and excretes darkness, spinning it in webs and an all-smothering night.

---

2 *Paradise Lost*, 1.60–64.
3 *Inferno* 3.22–24.

The death of a good man is not so, as the countenance reposes in peace, but the darkness of what should be alive but is a living death — the darkness of a soul that has handed itself over to evil — is dreadful to behold.

The story of mankind from the first Adam's waking into the world, to the last Adam's coming in glory, is just the story of that battleground between light and un-light. We all walk in the valley of the shadow of death (Ps. 23:4), and apart from Christ, the best we can do in our inner darkness is to approach the presence of God in timidity, divided from him by the veil that shadows him forth and shields us from his splendor. But when Christ died for us, that impetuous bridegroom tore the veil in two from top to bottom (Lk. 23:45), so that we who believe need no more veil, for "we all, with open face beholding as in a glass the glory of the Lord, are changed into the same image from glory to glory, even as by the Spirit of the Lord" (2 Cor. 3:18). We too enter the battle, and with a will, trusting in what the Lord has promised to those who hold fast and win the victory: "I will give him the morning star" (Rev. 2:28).

Indeed, the Light has shown itself forth, and poor, shriveling, time-bound, weakling darkness finds itself encompassed from the beginning and at the end. For the end is not darkness but Light.

6

There was a man sent from God, whose name was John.

"Lo, to prepare thy way,"
Did God the Father say,
"Before thy face my messenger I send,
Thy coming to forerun;
As on the orient sun
Doth the bright daystar morn by morn attend."[1]

WHAT AUTHORITY DID ADAM EXERCISE WHEN he named the beasts? We must not think of it as a random association of sounds with things. Man does not merely assign meaning. He sees meaning. He sees what a thing is, and he names it accordingly. That happens all through Scripture, and in fact a change of name signifies a change in being: so Jacob, the heel-grabbing twin who came forth from the womb hard upon his brother Esau, is called Yisroel, God perseveres, because he wrestled with the angel and did not give in (Gen. 32:28). Ezekiel foretells the return of Israel from their scattering at the hands of the Assyrians, and when they rebuild the holy city, its new name shall be Yahweh-shammah, The Lord is there (Ez. 48:35). So when Simon makes his daring confession of faith, Jesus renames him, as a sign that he is in some sense a new creation: "Thou art Peter, and upon this rock I will build my church" (Mt. 16:18; petrai).

So we should pay attention to the name John, rendered into Greek as Ioannes, but in Hebrew Yochanan, God is gracious. It is the name of the evangelist, who is shy of naming himself in his gospel and his letters, but who in the Apocalypse, meant for wide distribution, puts his name forward as an earnest of the truth of what he has seen. It is not a prominent name in the Old Testament. The most notable man to bear it is Johanan the son of Kareah, who avenged the assassination of the good man Gedaliah, whom

---

1 St. Bede the Venerable (673–735), *Praecursor altus luminis*, tr. C. S. Calverley.

God had appointed to govern the remnant of the people in Judah after the Babylonians had destroyed the Temple and taken most of the survivors into captivity. But when Johanan asked the prophet Jeremiah to pray to God for them, to tell them where they should go and what they should do, and Jeremiah said that they should remain in Judah, Johanan refused to believe him. Instead he took the people into Egypt, with Jeremiah his captive (Jer. 40 – 43). Not a promising name, then. We may reverse the order of God's name and the verb, and then we get *Hananiah* or *Ananias*, *Gracious is God*. That name, too, is associated with no one important — with one inauspicious exception. It is the happy-clappy prophet Hananiah, who gave the people false confidence, that God would break the yoke of the Babylonians. Said Jeremiah to him: "Hear now, Hananiah; the Lord hath not sent thee; but thou makest this people to trust in a lie" (Jer. 28:15). That John was not "sent" as a forerunner to anyone or anything.

So we might well understand why the kinfolk of Zachariah were puzzled when he and his wife Elizabeth named their child John: "And they said unto her, There is none of thy kindred that is called by this name" (Lk. 1:61). That might be the only reason why you would give a boy that name, if an uncle or cousin bore it. It named no hero. But Zachariah confirmed Elizabeth's choice: "And he asked for a writing table, and wrote, saying, His name is John" (Lk. 1:63).

I lay stress upon what was then an unusual name. The word for *grace*, in the Old Testament, is not common. It suggests a bending-down, a condescension of the superior to the inferior. Outside of poetry and prophecy, it is used exclusively in one sense: grace or favor *in someone's sight*. As such it is part of a formula, first used of Noah, who "found grace in the eyes of the Lord" (Gen. 6:8). When Boaz the wealthy farmer has pity upon Ruth, and invites her to glean in his fields only, she "fell on her face, and bowed herself to the ground, and said unto him, Why have I found grace in thine eyes, that thou shouldest take knowledge of me, seeing I am a stranger?" (Ru. 2:10).

But in the New Testament, the Greek *charis*, *grace*, and its relations are everywhere to be found. Think of the English word *eucharist*, *thanksgiving*. What has changed, from the Old Testament to the New? We might ask why it is fitting that a man with the name *God is gracious* should herald the coming of Christ. "All is grace," said Saint Thérèse of Lisieux. "But God commendeth his love toward us, in that, while we were yet sinners, Christ died for us," says Saint Paul (Rom. 5:8). It is the ultimate gift for the wholly undeserving, "for if through the offence of one many be dead, much more the grace of God, and the gift by grace, which is by one man, Jesus Christ, hath abounded unto many" (Rom. 5:15). Man ever wishes to *cut a deal* with God — a sense that underlies the Hebrew *berith*, *covenant*. Now, even in the Old Testament the symbolism of the Passover and the Day of Atonement suggested that the deal-cutting was a matter of God's gracious gift, and not a mutual exchange: of the two goats chosen for the Day of Atonement, the one that by lot is God's is sacrificed, while the "scapegoat," the one ritually identified with the sins of the whole people, is driven forth from their midst, alive (Lev. 16). But with Christ, all dickering with God is nailed to the Cross. Such dickering smacks of presumption, but we are to make manifest in our human way what Christ made manifest in *his divine and human way*, who, "being found in *fashion* as a man, he humbled himself, and became obedient unto death, even the death of the cross" (Phil. 2:8). "Peace I leave with you," says Jesus to the apostles at table on the dread night before his death, "my peace I give unto you: not as the world giveth, give I unto you" (Jn. 14:27).

So then, *there was a man sent from God, whose name was God is gracious.* The current Catholic lectionary, dead to the poetic, is nearly alone among reputable translations now current in burying the crucial name in the middle of the sentence and omitting the sentence's solemn opening. Here is their work: *A man named John was sent from God.* But the opening of the verse that John wrote — Greek *egeneto* — echoes that same word that he has already used for things that come to be. One of those things, in the providence of God, was the birth of the prophet John. And so we have here another example of that perichoretic narrative, with the resumption of motifs we have seen, and their being woven into a sentence with a new motif. Here the new motif is the *name*, which the evangelist will broach again, but not in the same context.

We see again, by the way, how important it is that the Greek *anthropos* be translated as *man* throughout, to bind the verses together. For the life that is the Word of God is the Light of *men*, as I have said — all together, and each one singly and personally, because, as Saint Paul will urge us to understand, each one of us is named Adam, and each one of us must put off that old man and put on the new man, who is Christ (cf. Eph. 4:21–24). God has chosen to save men through men, so there was a man sent from God, not an angel.

One final consideration: John *was sent*: Greek *apestolmenos*. That comes from one of the two principal words in the New Testament for sending:

the verb *apostellein*. We should hear that verb every time we see the word *apostle*: someone who has been dispatched with an important message to deliver. John the Baptist was thus the first great *apostle* in the life of Christ, and his message is ultimately what the evangelist says it is. Not the imparting of information, or a plan of action against the Romans. He points to Christ: Christ is himself the message. "Behold the Lamb of God, which taketh away the sins of the world," says John, alluding to the Passover lamb, sacrificed and eaten in memorial of the night when God slew the first-born of Egypt but spared the faithful children of Israel from death (Jn. 1:29). He is the prophet foretold by God to Malachi, whose name itself means *Messenger of the Lord*: "Behold, I will send my messenger and he shall prepare the way before me" (Mal. 3:1). If John was hearing Hebrew and Aramaic behind that important word *apostle*, we may think of the verb *shalach, to send*, but also *to shoot*: the *shelach* is a *weapon shot forth*, or a *shoot* from a tree. "*Send me*," says the prophet Isaiah to the Lord (7:8; Hebrew *shelacheni*). It is not always soft and sweet, that message shot from God.

7

The same came for a witness, to bear witness of the Light, that all men through him might believe.

Lord, how can man preach thy eternal word?
He is a brittle crazy glass:
Yet in thy temple thou dost him afford
This glorious and transcendent place,
To be a window, through thy grace. [1]

NOW THE EVANGELIST BROACHES TWO MOST important motifs, those of the *witness* and *belief*. They are intimately bound together: the witness is for the sake of belief. Notice that we are again enfolded in that braiding of motifs I have mentioned before, calling it perichoretic narrative: the Baptist (from verse 6) came for a *witness* (new motif), to bear *witness* (repeated, in altered form) of the *Light* (verses 4 and 5), that all men might *believe* (new motif) *through* (verse 3) him.

The noun for the act of witnessing is Greek *martyria*, from the noun *martys*, witness; the verb is *martyrein*. Again, we stand on the brink of a chasm in the history of mankind. Whenever the sacred authors of the Old Testament write about a man's *witness* and *testimony*, the context is legal, either in fact or by analogy. So did Abraham set apart seven ewe lambs for Abimelech "that they may be a witness" (Gen. 21:30), to settle a dispute over the well that Abraham had dug and that Abimelech's servants had taken by violence. So did God demand that there be two or three witnesses to swear that a man had committed a crime punishable by death, "but at the mouth of one witness he shall not be put to death" (Dt. 17:6). Job in his misery says that his friends with their accusations have creased his face with wrinkles, "which is a witness against me: and my leanness rising up

---

1   George Herbert, from "The Windows."

in me beareth witness to my face" (Jb. 16:8). We can certainly find in the Old Testament the reality of martyrdom as Christians understand it, but as yet there is no word for it, and no clear conception of it.

The *martyr* in the special and elevated sense in which Saint John uses the word is one who will testify to the truth with his very life, laying that life on the line, and accepting death with courage and gratitude, to say, "I have seen this, I testify to it, and I will die for it." To save their skins, the Greek and Roman pagans of John's time would have denied the truth of every story about Zeus and Apollo and Aphrodite and all their fellows and all their rabble of subordinate gods; and then the more superstitious among them at the first opportunity would have gone to a temple for expiation. I am not saying that they did not believe those stories. I am saying that the willingness to die for the truth of God, to be a witness who would accept death rather than deny that Jesus Christ died and rose from the dead on the third day, is a new thing in the world. The new thing is among us still, as Christians in Armenia, Tunisia, Algeria, Nigeria, and the Sudan testify. The mere boy José Sánchez del Río went to the firing squad in Mexico, while sophisticated Americans of the left gave their hesitant approval to the forces of social enlightenment who swung the rifles. His captors promised to spare him if only he would say, "Death to Christ the King!" They had mocked him and cut his feet and slashed him with machetes, but the boy would not give in. "¡Viva Cristo Rey!" he cried. Then they shot him.

Almost every time we read of a *witness* or a *testimony* in the New Testament, we should think of a *martyr* in that special and tremendous sense. "We also are compassed about," says he who writes to the Hebrews, "with so great a cloud of *martyrs*" (Heb. 12:1). "Ye are *martyrs* of these things," says the risen Christ to his apostles, sending them forth to preach to all nations (Lk. 24:48). Christ himself is "the faithful *martyr*, and the first begotten of the dead" (Rev. 1:5; cf. Ps. 89:37). This again is for John a much-treasured word; its forms appear in his gospel, his letters, and the Apocalypse 59 times. See the beginning of his first letter, "for the life was manifested, and we have seen it, and *bear witness*, and show unto you that eternal life, which was with the Father, and was manifested unto us" (1 Jn. 1:2; note the braiding). See also the beginning of the Apocalypse: "The [Apocalypse] of Jesus Christ, which God gave unto him, to shew unto his servants things which must shortly come to pass; and he sent and signified it by his angel unto his servant John: who bare record of the word of God, and of the *testimony* of Jesus Christ, and of all things that he saw" (Rev. 1:1−2; if you read farther, you will note the braiding here too).

But in the gospels we find also the *false witness*, the *pseudomartyr*. The difference between the martyr and the pseudomartyr is not simply the difference between true and false testimonies. The whole dramatic situation is different. "Now the chief priests, and elders, and all the council," says Matthew, "sought *false witness* against Jesus, to put him to death" (Mt. 26:59; Greek *pseudomartyrian*). But though many people came forth with their lies, they could not find the cause they sought, until "at the last came two *false witnesses*, And said, This fellow said, I am able to destroy the temple of God, and to build it in three days" (60 − 61). The false witness, the pseudomartyr, lays *his enemy's life* on the line. He testifies to a lie to put to death the man he hates. The true witness, the true martyr, dies for the truth, out of love even for those who hate him.

The *false witness* in Hebrew is the *'ed chamas*, literally the *violent witness*, the *witness to do injury*. Such a false witness is an adversary, an accuser, a *satan*: so to punish the apostasy of Solomon, God "stirred him up another *adversary*, Rezon the son of Eliadah" (1 Kg. 11:23; Hebrew *satan*). The great adversary, Satan, "was a murderer from the beginning, and abode not in the truth," says Jesus (Jn. 8:44). He slanders to kill.

The English word *witness*, unlike its Greek and Hebrew counterparts, has to do with *seeing and knowing*, as in being *wise*, and having your *wits* about you. Jesus does not have to see to believe, since he is himself the object of belief, though in his words and his deeds he shows to others who he is. It is the Father himself who bears witness:

> If I bear witness of myself, my witness is not true.
>
> There is another that beareth witness of me; and I know that the witness which he witnesseth of me is true.
>
> Ye sent unto John, and he bare witness unto the truth.
>
> But I receive not testimony from man: but these things I say, that ye may be saved.
>
> He was a burning and a shining light: and ye were willing for a season to rejoice in his light.
>
> But I have a greater witness than that of John: for the works which the Father hath given me to finish, the same works that I do, bear witness of me, that the Father hath sent me. (Jn. 5:31−36)

Always we return to the question, who do we say Jesus is? Saint John bears witness to things he saw, in order to bear witness to who Jesus is,

49

the only-begotten Son of God, "which we have seen with our eyes, which we have looked upon, and our hands have handled, of the Word of life" (1 Jn. 1:1), whom we too must believe in, because "behold, he cometh with clouds; and every eye shall see him" (Rev. 1:7). When Caiaphas the high priest demanded that Jesus declare himself, "whether thou be Christ, the Son of God," he did not actually want to know. Caiaphas wanted Jesus to condemn himself, because he assumed from the outset that he knew the answer to the question. Jesus could have saved himself perhaps by evasion or false witness, but he spoke the truth: "Hereafter shall ye see the Son of man sitting on the right hand of power, and coming in the clouds of heaven." At which the high priest tore his clothes and said, "What further need have we of *witnesses?*" (Mt. 26:63 – 65; Greek *martyron*).

John the Baptist was sent by God, then, that *through him* all those he witnessed to — unto the loss of his own life — might *believe*, or, as Monsignor Ronald Knox has it in his suggestive though idiosyncratic translation, might *learn to believe*. What does this mean, to *believe?* I cannot write here an entire treatise on Christian faith. But there are a few things I should like to note, things that may be obscured by the double translation into our English from the Hebrew or Aramaic upon Jesus's lips and in John's memory, and from the Greek he wrote down as he thought in terms as stark and clear as he could make them.

We must hold together at once, and allow them to shed light on one another, those places in the New Testament that speak of *belief, faith*, and *trustworthiness*, along with every instance in which Jesus utters the Hebrew word *amen*, translated sometimes as *truly* or *verily*, and sometimes left as is. The Hebrew root verb, *'aman*, means to *confirm*, to *support*, as a pillar, or as the source of your sustenance. It is *firm and sure*. We find its adverbial form *amen* in sacred formulas in the Old Testament: "So be it, O Lord," says the prophet Jeremiah, when God sends him to remind the people of Judah of the covenant he made with their fathers, to bring them into a land flowing with milk and honey (Jer. 11:5; Hebrew *amen*). We find it also in doxologies, glory-words: "Blessed be the Lord God of Israel from everlasting, and to everlasting. Amen, and Amen" (Ps. 41:13).

I put special stress upon *amen*, because it is a startling feature of Jesus's speech, and one that we are likely to overlook, because we have become too familiar with it. Any of us might say, "I'm telling you the truth here," urging someone to believe us, and often without success. Jesus does more than that. When he *precedes* his sayings with *amen*, as he does several dozen times in the gospels, he is asserting something about himself, just as he does when he goes beyond the law of Moses, even correcting that law when it was but a concession to the hardness of men's hearts. He is teaching "as one that had authority" (Mk. 1:22), that is, as one who gives the law rather than merely interpreting it or calling upon what the teachers of old had to say about it. The Greek there for *authority* is *exousia*, literally, that which proceeds *from one's being*. We can attribute authority to a man by his office, or by his position in a natural hierarchy, or perhaps by his natural gifts, but only to God do we attribute authority unequivocally. He who demands to be trusted, to be believed in, is himself the authority, and he himself says *amen*: "I am alive for evermore, Amen" (Rev. 1:18).

To fail to believe in Jesus is not to fail at an opinion. The gods, says the poet Lucan, who harbored republican sympathies during the reign of Nero when it was dangerous to do so, favored the cause of Julius Caesar in the Roman civil war, but the virtuous Cato favored Pompey, as did Lucan himself. That is not like what we do when we respond to Jesus by turning aside. It would seem unjust if God were to condemn us for being fallible in what we think. The failure to believe is more profound. It is to fall into an abyss. If Jesus is the Amen, rather than merely someone whom we happen to trust, then we must throw ourselves upon his saving power, because nothing and no one else will suffice. There is no foundation upon which man can build, says Saint Paul, other than Jesus Christ (1 Cor. 3:11). "There is none other name under heaven given among men," said Saint Peter, mere days after the Holy Spirit descended upon him and the other apostles, "whereby we must be saved" (Acts 4:12). How this faith may be made manifest among men who have not heard of the name of Jesus, or to whom Jesus has not been clearly preached, I will not say. I leave that matter to the providential justice and mercy of God. But when you are falling to your death, it does not matter what you may think about this or that streamer floating in the wind. Grab hold of the streamer all you want. It will not save you. There is only one name in which we may be saved, one lifeline thrown out to us. Lifelines of the imagination vanish between our fingers.

8

He was not that Light, but was
sent to bear witness of that Light.

Jesus, our only joy be thou,
As thou our prize wilt be;
In thee be all our glory now,
And through eternity.[1]

THE EMPHASIS HERE IS ON *HE*, IN GREEK
ekeinos, that man there, and on *not,* which is the first word in John's
sentence. Jerome's Latin preserves the word order nicely, along
with the demonstrative pronoun: *Non erat ille lux, not was that man the light.*

There is no verb in the Greek. We have an elliptic sentence, perhaps to
be construed closely with the previous sentence as one extended expression.
Why would John include it at all? What does it add to what we already
have been told?

The evangelist is at pains to emphasize two things. One is that John
was sent to bear witness *to* the Light, and the other is that he himself was
not the Light. The second is not implied by the first. Jesus came, and he
did testify to himself; but John is always pointing away from himself,
and forward. "He must increase, but I must decrease," says he (Jn. 3:30),
meaning that Christ must grow in greatness, while he, John, becomes
small. That is John's impressive humility. Jesus is the only man who can
say, pointing to himself without contradiction, "Take my yoke upon you,
and learn of me; for I am meek and lowly in heart" (Mt. 11:29).

The Baptist is an important strand in the divine braiding of time. When
the Jews *sent* (Greek *apesteilan*; God sends, and so does man) priests and
Levites from Jerusalem to ask the Baptist who he was, they must have been
looking for the Messiah, because John's reply is, "I am not the Christ" (Jn.
1:20). They will ask him why he is doing what he is doing, but their first
question has to do with identity and with the providential and saving plan

---

1 From *Jesu, dulcis memoria,* 12th c.; trans. Edward Caswall, 1849.

of God. Hence John finally replies, in a verse that all the evangelists cite: "I am the voice of one crying in the wilderness, Make straight the way of the Lord, as said the prophet Esaias" (1:23; cf. Is. 40:3). It is a prophecy of Messianic fulfillment, for "the glory of the Lord shall be revealed, and all flesh shall see it together" (Is. 40:5).

So the Baptist in his moment looks back upon the prophet Isaiah, in order to locate that prophecy both in the here and now and in time to come. It is and is not like when Jesus reads from the same prophet, proclaiming comfort to those who mourn, liberty to captives, and pardon to prisoners, and he says, simply and boldly, "This day is this scripture fulfilled in your ears" (Lk. 4:21; cf. Is. 61:1–2). It is *not* like it, because John affirms of himself only the status of the forerunner, while Jesus affirms not merely that he is *going to fulfill* the prophecy of Isaiah, but that he *has already fulfilled it*. That affirmation makes sense as more than a brazen figure of speech only if we notice that it is bolder still: Jesus claims *to be its fulfillment*, in his very person. We want from Jesus, finally, what no Greek wanted from Zeus, no Viking wanted from Odin, no Muslim wants from Mohammed, nor even any Buddhist wants from the Buddha. We want Jesus himself; as the Psalmist cries to the Lord, "Thou art my refuge and my portion in the land of the living" (Ps. 142:5). "You have written well of me, Thomas," said the Lord to Thomas Aquinas once when he was celebrating Mass, and he asked him what he wanted from him in return. "*Non nisi te*," said Thomas — "none else but thee."

What the Baptist says is like what Jesus says, because it requires us to dwell in more than one mode of time at once, without either mode passing away. This habit of seeing the past in the future and the future in the past and both past and future as urgently present is characteristic both of what the evangelist John says, and of the way he says it. "I baptize with water," says the Anticipator, "but there standeth one among you, whom ye know not; He it is, who coming after me is preferred before me" (Jn. 1:26–27). To Nathanael, Jesus says, "Before that Philip called thee, when thou wast under the fig tree, I saw thee," and then, when Nathanael marvels and says that Jesus is the King of Israel — the King who is, and who is to come, since Jesus is but a man before Nathanael's eyes, and not robed in a royal gown — Jesus replies, "Thou shalt see greater things than these" (1:48–50). When the Jews ask Jesus for a sign, to justify his casting the moneychangers out of the Temple, Jesus says, "Destroy this temple, and in three days I will raise it up" (Jn. 2:19). That causes the Jews to think back upon the forty-six years it took to build that temple, but Jesus "spake of the temple of his body," as his disciples would remember, after he had risen from the dead (20 – 21). "The hour is coming, and now is," says Jesus, "when the dead shall hear the voice of the Son of God: and they that hear shall live" (5:25). "But the hour cometh, and now is," he says to the Samaritan woman at the well (who has challenged him first by recalling "our father Jacob," and then by referring to "our fathers" who worshiped on the mountain and not in Jerusalem), "when the true worshippers shall worship the Father in spirit and in truth" (4:24). "Yet a little while, and the world seeth me no more," he says to his disciples at the Last Supper, "but ye see me: because I live, ye shall live also" (14:19).

Perhaps the apostle who was closest to Jesus, the lad who was all ears, who best caught the soul within the patterns of his speech, can best tell us about time and eternity, and do so in poetic language that is in one sense simple, because its vocabulary is so straightforward, as I have said, but in another sense comprehensive, with the simplicity of fullness and completion. Let us think about this for a moment. We are accustomed to stories that begin at a certain point, usually with a problem, and that work their way toward triumph or tragedy or, if you are many a modern author, an anti-triumph that yet makes some kind of declaration. Look at the stories man tells about himself. The people of Athens, with Athena casting the tiebreaking vote, acquit Orestes of murder, but the goddess invites the prosecuting Furies to look kindly upon the city, and when they agree, when they set aside their agony and vindictiveness, they become the Eumenides, the Kindly Ones. That is how Aeschylus, the most pious of the Greek tragedians, gives us the history of mankind proceeding from blood vengeance and pride, to justice meted out by a community of free men, men who still honor the old bonds of blood. Man ascends and becomes an Athenian. Or, to fall a bit from the sublime, people wrest their sustenance from a forbidding land, and gradually free themselves from darkness and superstition, giving themselves entirely to technology, so that they finally invent tractors, and all is well. Man ascends and becomes Henry Ford. Or, to fall farther, he invents synthetic estrogen, and becomes a liberated woman with a mortgage and no children. Call it progressive quicksand. The story goes somewhere, but the somewhere does not satisfy. We long not for progress but for transcendence, that which alone makes any sense of progress.

In the Christian story alone, and here I include the whole story of the children of Israel and the far-seeing and inward-enlightening visions

54

of the prophets, do we find progress and return, consummation hidden in what is no bigger than a mustard seed, transcendence in the unseen action of a little yeast. I mean that here and here alone are all these things true at once: the story of mankind is the story of each man, singly, and really, not figuratively; mankind and each man has a beginning, and the end he strives for is already incorporated in that beginning; the end does not obliterate the beginning, but recovers it and redeems it and raises it to glory; and the end, a new heaven and a new earth, is among us now, but is not yet, and is in the flesh, yet a flesh that is as absolute light by comparison with the shadows we bear about with us.

If your soul has been washed in the blood of that story, and you have meditated upon it and upon the Man who is the answer to that story, its origin, its force, and its end — "I am the resurrection, and the life," says the Lord (Jn. 11:25) — you might write as John does, and John writes that way not because of any artistic excellence he naturally possesses. Again I stress this point. If John's gospel is great art, it is great art forged under the immense pressure of a great truth seen, heard, and touched. No narrative from any other culture is like this one. No story can conceivably be greater, and that, and not pride or defensiveness, is why he of the Apocalypse can say, "For I testify unto every man that heareth the words of the prophecy of this book. If any man shall add unto these things, God shall add unto him the plagues that are written in this book: And if any man shall take away from the words of the book of this prophecy, God shall take away his part out of the book of life, and out of the holy city, and from the things which are written in this book" (Rev. 22:18 – 19).

9

That was the true Light...

O brightness of the immortal Father's face,
Most holy, heavenly, blest,
Lord Jesus Christ, in whom his truth and grace
Are visibly expressed![1]

INTO THE PERICHORESIS COMES ANOTHER NEW
and tremendously important motif: the Light is *true*.

I have heard people say, with a great show of tolerance, that they
can live with my being a Christian if the story of Jesus "works" for me.
They may believe they mean well, but — to hell with tolerance of that
sort. I prefer the wisdom of Flannery O'Connor's Misfit, in "A Good Man
is Hard to Find." He is the Christ-haunted murderer who says he wishes
he had been in Jerusalem when they say Jesus rose from the dead, to see
if he did it or not. If he did it, then, says the Misfit, there's nothing for it
but to go sell all you have and follow him; but if he didn't, then there's
nothing for it but to rob and kill and do all kinds of meanness, getting
what little pleasure there is to get out of life. I do not say "Amen" to any
mere human story. "Put not your trust in princes," says the psalmist, "nor
in the son of man, in whom there is no help" (Ps. 146:3).

Jesus himself leaves us no way out. We must decide. He alone can free
us from sin. He alone brings us before the time of Moses, before the time
of Abraham, before the time of Adam and his fall. So he says to those who
would not believe him:

> If God were your Father, ye would love me; for I proceeded forth
> and came from God; neither came I myself, but he sent me.
>
> Why do ye not understand my speech? even because ye cannot
> hear my word.
>
> Ye are of your father the devil, and the lusts of your father ye
> will do. He was a murderer from the beginning, and abode not

---

1   *Phos hilaron*, 3rd c.; trans. Edward W. Eddis, 1864.

in the truth, because there is no truth in him. When he speaketh
a lie, he speaketh it of his own: for he is a liar, and the father of
it. (Jn. 8:42–44)

Jesus brings us here to the crisis of man. At every moment, we may follow the liar, the devil in his form as serpent — all mouth and alimentary
canal. We may believe the double lie, that God wishes to keep us low and
mean, and that we shall not die the death if we seize to our own deter-
mination what shall be called good and what shall be called evil (Gen.
3:4). To the Hebrew mind, a prophecy that does not come to pass is not
just a bad guess, unfulfilled. It is a lie. What God gives to the prophet in
a vision "shall speak, and not lie" (Hab. 2:3). If we trust in God and give
to those who hunger, says Isaiah, we shall "be like a watered garden, and
like a spring of water, whose waters fail not" (Is. 58:11) — literally, whose
waters *do not lie*.

We want truth, not lies. Even liars want *other people* to tell them the
truth, as thieves want to keep their property. Man thrives upon truth. "If a
son shall ask bread of any of you that is a father," says Jesus, "will he give
him a stone? or if he ask for a fish, will he for a fish give him a serpent?"
(Lk. 11:11). The stone is a lie, whether we pretend it is bread or not. The
serpent is a killer, no matter that we call it a fish. "My flesh," says Jesus, "is
true food, and my blood is true drink" (Jn. 6:55, translation mine). Even
the manna from heaven had not the truth, the utter trustworthiness, of
the bread of Christ, because it satisfied only for a time: "Your fathers ate
what-is-this in the wilderness, and are dead" (Jn. 6:49; translation mine).
The new *what-is-this*, the new *manna*, is true in an ultimate sense, because,
says Jesus, "whoso eateth my flesh and drinketh my blood hath eternal
life; and I will raise him up on the last day" (Jn. 6:54).

I do not think that man exactly *wants* to hear those words. The Jewish
leaders did not want to hear them. But what we wish were true and what
is true very often have little to do with one another. The Light that John
names is the *true Light*, and not just some light that happens to be true in
this or that respect. It is true because it comes from God, and it is in fact
God. "I hate and abhor lying," says the psalmist, "but thy law do I love"
(Ps. 119:163). The true prophets had far more unwelcome things to say
to the people than the people cared for. The words of false prophets had
the flash and glare of an *ignis fatuus* glowing above a swamp, but people
will follow such words, "and no marvel," says Saint Paul, speaking of
false apostles, deceitful workers, "for Satan himself is transformed into an

angel of light" (2 Cor. 11:13 – 14). The flash and glare of the liar is thus the inverse of the Son of God whose glory is hidden, even in swaddling clothes as he lies in the manger.

What does it mean to be *true*? Let us follow up on suggestions provided by our three languages in play, Hebrew, Greek, and English. In the Hebrew, as we have seen, truth is associated with firmness, solidity, reliability, as of a rock. Imagine a man climbing the side of a rock face. He sends a searching foot to his right for a sure toe-hold, but it is a *false move*, as we say. What seems to be a sure abutment of stone is deceptive, as loose as shale, and it crumbles at a touch. You cannot climb the mountain of life by pretending.

In Greek, *aletheia*, *truth*, is candid, not secretive, open, not sly, present to the mind, not buried in forgetfulness. Any ordinary speaker of Greek as a second or third language would have been aware of these associations: cf. Greek *lethe*, *forgetfulness*. This light is for all men, and not to be smuggled away and enjoyed only by the few, as was the "light" provided by the so-called mystery cults of the Hellenistic world, cults wherein the initiate would be introduced to knowledge that had to be kept secret. Jesus was exposed upon the cross, naked to all the world. "For there is nothing covered," says Jesus, "that shall not be revealed; neither hid, that shall not be known" (Lk. 12:2), and so did Saint Peter leave the huddle of the upper room to proclaim the risen Christ from the housetop (Acts 2).

English gives us a third sense: that of *being straight*, firmly so, like a *tree*. We say of a marksman that his aim is *true*: it does not sway up or down, to left or to right. We say of a wall that it is *true*: the corners are right-angled, and the wall stands plumb. "*Guai a voi, anime prave!*" cries Charon the ferryman of the dead to the souls of the newly damned, in Dante's poem — "*Woe to you, you crooked souls!*" (*Inf.* 3.84). Sin makes man bent, says Saint Augustine, citing the psalmist: "Their eyes are darkened lest they see, and their backs are hunched over" (Ps. 68:24; translation mine). "What wonder is it," he says, "when they who prostrate themselves for earthly things and never look up toward those of heaven, should have the back always bent?" (*The City of God*, 17.19; Latin *incurvum*). We are cripples. It needs the grace of God to straighten us out, to make us good and true.

We might put together these three insights into what is true as they apply to man in our time. He is willing to grant truth to inanimate things, truth that can be determined by the methods of empirical investigation and measurement. When he refuses to grant that truth applies to moral action, or to the existence of God, or to the story of God's salvific involvement in human history, he trammels up the truth, and in so doing he trammels up himself. He locks himself in a cell and will not surrender the key. Inevitably he looks to find his good in *things*, in the objects of hedonistic lust, avarice, or ambition. Materialism in philosophy implies materialism in act. Jesus says that the truth shall set us free (Jn. 8:32). The beginning of freedom is to confess that truth exists. The truth-denier claps the fetters on his own feet. He is a slave to every social fad produced by the engines of mass opinion and mass entertainment. This he calls progress.

...which lighteth every man that cometh into the world.

Christ, whose glory fills the skies,
Christ, the true, the only Light,
Sun of Righteousness, arise!
Triumph o'er the shades of night:
Dayspring from on high, be near;
Daystar, in my heart appear.[2]

MORE BRAIDING: THE MOTIF OF MAN returns (not just *everyone*, as the New American Bible renders it, smothering the specific and personal and breaking the poetic connections), along with the repeated *light*. The latter, here, is doubtless a typical noun-verb doublet in John's Semitic imagination: *the light enlightens, ha-'ur ya'ir*. Then comes the new motif, that of *the world*: Greek *kosmos*, translating Hebrew *tebel*. The Hebrew word is common in the Psalms and Isaiah: "For the world is mine," says God, "and the fullness thereof" (Ps. 50:12). It suggests *totality*, which otherwise would be described by "heaven and earth," or "the heavens and the earth." Latin *universum* is similar: literally, *everything rolled up into one*.

The Greek word *kosmos* is somewhat different. It suggests what is *orderly, decorous, beautiful*, with all things set just so; cf. English *cosmetics*. Let the women, says Saint Paul, "*adorn* themselves in *modest* apparel" (1 Tim. 2:9; *kosmein, kosmioi*). When the ancient Greeks, who with the Chinese seem

---

2   John Wesley, 1740.

to have been a people peculiarly susceptible to beauty, looked upon the world about them, they saw order, and they thought it was their task to imitate that order in their arts, and study that order in their sciences, and contemplate that order in their pursuit of wisdom. I do not suggest that the Hebrews saw disorder; far from it. Says the Lord out of the whirl-wind, speaking to Job: "Hast thou commanded the morning since thy days; and caused the dayspring to know his place?" (Job 34:12). But the Hebrews did not really look upon the world as if it possessed beauty of its own, apart from God. The beauty led them to ask, rather, about the Creator of that beauty, and man's relationship to him. Says the psalmist:

> When I consider thy heavens, the work of thy fingers, the moon
> and the stars, which thou hast ordained;
>   What is man, that thou art mindful of him? and the son of
> man, that thou visitest him?
>   For thou hast made him a little lower than the angels, and hast
> crowned him with glory and honor. (Ps. 8:3–5)

The Greeks, bound by their paganism, never did make the passage from believing in a god-in-the-cosmos to the God who made the cosmos, freely, without any necessity, as an overflowing gift of his goodness and his existence. Their cosmos was, shall we say, cosmetic. It did not in itself enter into an adventure of being-created by the gods from nothing, and being destined to return to the gods. It simply was what it was. For the Greek, it was home.

For John, so sunny a view of the world was not possible, because it was not true. Always in John, *the world* is a fallen world, involved in the drama of sinful man who was created for goodness but who by his own sin devoted himself to death. We Christians must maintain a double view of the world. It is the swarming place of lies. It is the market of false prophets, who say that Jesus Christ did not come in the flesh. Such men are in the world, and "are of the world: therefore speak they of the world, and the world heareth them" (1 Jn. 4:5). It is the proscenium of ambition; but, says Saint Paul, "God forbid that I should glory, save in the cross of our Lord Jesus Christ, by whom the world is crucified unto me, and I unto the world" (Gal. 6:14). It is the open sore of care and trouble, where "the sorrow of the world worketh death" (2 Cor. 7:10). It is the grave of disappointment and futility: "For what shall it profit a man, if he shall gain the whole world, and lose his own soul?" (Mk. 8:36). Yet in spite of it all, it is still God's world, and "God so loved the world, that he gave his only begotten Son, that whosoever believeth in him should not perish, but have everlasting life" (Jn. 3:16).

Nevertheless, we must reckon with the *world*, one of the most important words and ideas in both Saint John and Saint Paul. It has entered into the Christian consciousness that we must be in the world yet not *of the world*: so says Jesus in his high-priestly prayer for the apostles on the night before his death: "I have given them thy word; and the world hath hated them, because they are not of the world, even as I am not of the world" (Jn. 17:14). The world — with its characteristic sins of avarice and social climbing — is one of the trio of tempters that Christians had considered as covering all conceivable sins: the world, the flesh, and the devil. So Christians have had to join in Christ's work of redeeming the world by preaching him, by living public lives that are sharply distinct from those of the worldlings about them, and sometimes by leaving the world behind, to live in solitude, or in a communion of men or women set apart in a monastery. The world does not understand such actions, but we should expect no better, when "God hath chosen the foolish things of the world to confound the wise; and God hath chosen the weak things of the world to confound the things which are mighty" (1 Cor. 1:27).

We are thus always enjoined to enter more fully and bravely into the real history of the world, which is the story of man's salvation, wholly the work of Christ and therefore also the work of those in whom Christ works, and who become more truly themselves by it — or rather become themselves for the first time after all. Sometimes that means that we do what the world finds baffling, such as the young poet and scholar George Herbert did, leaving behind a promising career in London to become the curate of a far-flung parish in the moorlands and swamplands of Kent. "The world and I will quarrel," he promises Christ in "The Thanksgiving," "and the year / Shall not perceive that I am here" (37–38). Even people who are not thinking specifically of the Christian life will feel the burden of a life in the "world," as Saint John intends it. "The world is too much with us," says William Wordsworth, thinking of a life wholly given up to industry and moneymaking, as "getting and spending, we lay waste our powers." "All the world's a stage," says Shakespeare's cynical Jacques, "and all the men and women merely players."

I do not need to give witness that life given up to the "world" is on a highway to disappointment and exhaustion. The worldly themselves testify.

The atheist of our time does not rejoice in the beauty of the world around us, a beauty which might lead him to the threshold of faith. Instead he lays stress upon what he sees as its cruelty, its wastage, its ugliness, its unmeaning. The cosmos for him is no longer a *cosmos* but a *chaos*. The amoralist of our time does not rejoice in the beauty of the natural virtues, a beauty he does not feel. Instead he insists that there are no such things at all, so that he may indulge himself in vices that a healthy people would consider disgusting, unsightly, base, and abominable. Every one of our arts has reeled back into the beast. It appears that to love the created world as it deserves to be loved, man must not demand from it what only God can give. Man must not be of the world, if for no other reason than that he might love the world he is in. "Seek ye the kingdom of God," says Jesus, "and all these things shall be added unto you" (Lk. 12:31).

One last point about the word "world" in translations of the New Testament. Every time the Greek *kosmos* appears, it will be rendered as "world," but not every "world" renders the Greek *kosmos*. Sometimes it is the Greek *aion*, meaning *age* or *era*. From that word, archaeologists and historians coined the English *eon*, to signify a vast stretch of time. We have had also a very old and distant cousin of the Greek word in the archaic English *aye*, meaning not *yes* — the *aye* that means *yes* is a different word entirely, and the identical spelling is merely coincidental — but *ever*, as in the fossil-phrase *for aye*, *forever*. The point is that this *aion*, this age or world, is passing away, and it is foolish to bow down to what is passing as if it were eternal. "Be not conformed to this *world*," says Saint Paul, "but be ye transformed by the renewing of your mind" (Rom. 12:2; Greek *aioni*). If we leave all that we love for the sake of the kingdom of God, says Jesus, we shall receive "manifold more in this present time, and in the *world* to come life *everlasting*" (Lk. 18:30; Greek *aioni, aionion*). The truth of the Lord, says the psalmist, endures *eis ton aiona, unto the age*, that is, *unto the eternal* (Ps. 116:2; Septuagint).

10

He was in the world, and the world was made by him, and the world knew him not.

Some said, that I the Temple to the floor
In three days razed, and raised as before.
Why, he that built the world can do much more:
Was ever grief like mine?[1]

WITH THIS VERSE, DRAMATIC IRONY ENTERS the gospel of John. It is dramatic irony on a cosmic scale. What greater ignorance can there be, than that the very creator of the world should enter the world as a creature, and that the world, his own creation, should not know him? Thus we find that inversion of the world's values and expectations which is the true mark of a Christian view of time and of the course of human life.

John has raised to the ultimate degree an irony foreshadowed in the history of the chosen people of God, whom God saves when they least expect it and by means they would not have found for themselves. Consider the means: the exile Moses, living a quiet life in the grasslands far from the bustle of Egypt; the young lad David, whom his father Jesse nearly forgot about when Samuel came to anoint one of his sons; the prophet Jeremiah, hated by the pious leaders in Jerusalem; the baby Joash, hidden away from the hatred of Athaliah, but destined to be king of Israel after her sudden and violent downfall; even Abraham, old and matched with a barren wife, a stranger in a strange land, from whose loins nevertheless will come and have come descendants as countless as the grains of sand on the seashore.

Throughout the New Testament, this irony of reversing the expectations of man appears in what Jesus says, in what he does, and in who he

---

1 From George Herbert, "The Sacrifice" (69–72).

is. "Blessed are the meek," he says, "for they shall inherit the earth" (Mt. 5:5). The meek? Those who do not sweat and strain to reach the heights of wealth and power? "If any man desire to be first," he says, when his disciples were bickering about which among them would be the greatest in the kingdom of God, "the same shall be last of all, and servant of all" (Mk. 9:35; and the Greek *doulos* might as easily be translated as *slave*). "And he took a child," Mark continues, "and set him in the midst of them: and when he had taken him in his arms, he said unto them, Whosoever shall receive one of such children in my name, receiveth me: and whosoever shall receive me, receiveth not me, but him that sent me" (Mk. 9:36–37). John, who according to tradition was the youngest of the apostles, and whom Christian artists have long portrayed as still with a boy's cheek and chin, must have taken that action and those words to heart, because in his letters he so often calls by a most affectionate address those he has baptized: "Ye are of God, little children, and have overcome them: because greater is he that is in you, than he that is in the world" (1 Jn. 4:4). Says the poet Herbert:

> Although by stealth
> My flesh get on, yet let her sister
> My soul bid nothing, but preserve her wealth;
> The growth of flesh is but a blister;
> Childhood is health. [2]

Small is the crawlway that leads to eternal life, and only little children can wriggle through it.

Who, then, is Jesus? He comes among us first as *the child Jesus*. The maker of all this world came into the world: the Creator himself, says Dante, in praise of the Virgin Mary, became "the creature of his creature" (*Paradiso* 33.3). John Donne fairly revels in the dramatic reversals of what man might expect. From his "Annunciation," addressing Mary:

> Ere by the spheres time was created, thou
> Wast in his mind, who is thy Son, and Brother;
> Whom thou conceiv'st, conceived; yea thou art now
> Thy Maker's maker, and thy Father's mother;
> Thou hast light in dark, and shutst in little room
> Immensity cloistered in thy dear womb. (9–14)

---

2 "Holy Baptism" (II), 11–15.

It may be a whimsical thing if Henry Ford were to show up unannounced at one of his company's factories far from Detroit, wearing ordinary overalls and pretending to be a hayseed, asking questions of the men working at the assembly lines, and finding out things from them that he could never have found out from officials who keep their jobs by making everything appear to be running smoothly. Whimsy is not in play here in John's gospel. That is not only because the stakes are heaven and earth.

There are at least two *moral* reasons why man does not recognize God, and the two are related. One is that God is too great for him, and the other is that God is too small. Let me explain.

The first thing that man does when he falls from grace is to hide. God calls to Adam, who says, "I heard thy voice in the garden, and I was afraid, because I was naked; and I hid myself" (Gen. 3:10). Milton can show us how the original sin was a fall from that communion with God which man should have found both tremendous and yet a sweet and daily thing, so long as he was innocent and dwelt within the haven of gratitude. Says the Son to the man who hides:

> My voice thou oft hast heard, and hast not feared,
> But still rejoiced; how is it now become
> So dreadful to thee? that thou art naked, who
> Hath told thee? hast thou eaten of the Tree
> Whereof I gave thee charge thou shouldst not eat? [3]

The irony, as I have shown above, is that Adam *was clothed* before the sin, clothed in honor and innocence. So did he stride forth in Eden to meet the angel Raphael, who has descended from the heavenly heights to dine with him and to warn him of the coming of a secret foe:

> Meanwhile our Primitive great Sire, to meet
> His god-like Guest, walked forth, without more train
> Accompanied than with his own complete
> Perfections; in himself was all his state. (5.350 – 53)

The innocent man needs neither shield nor disguise. He wears a robe of integrity. Once that robe is rent in two, he finds himself naked, and therefore he needs to cower and cringe. He is made in God's image, but he has befouled the divine in himself, and he no longer recognizes it there. They who dwell in tunnels and warrens can hardly bear to look upon the sun.

---

3   *Paradise Lost*, 10.119 – 23.

Their shoulders are puny, and a mere touch of the weighty glory of God will crush them like bugs.

But it is characteristic of the craven to turn from true greatness and to fall down in worship of its impostor, mere bigness. And in this sense God is too small for man. In Genesis, the turn toward bigness comes straightaway. Lamech boasts that he has outdone Cain and killed seven men instead of only one. The builders of the tower of Babel want to scratch the very firmament of heaven, with domination over their neighbors a fine bonus added into the bargain. The kings of Sodom and Gomorrah must rely upon Abram to save their hides, but Abram will not take a shoe-latch from any of them in reward. These kings and their soon to be obliterated cities prepare us for the power of Egypt looming ahead, and the proud Pharaoh who "knew not Joseph" (Ex. 1:8). Him God must humiliate, striking against the "god" on the throne by plagues that make jest of everything that the Egyptians most cherish, or believe divine, not least among them the sacred river Nile, whose waters God turns to blood.

Man with the soul of a child might find God in the form of a child, but man the swaggerer and bully, the coward rising a-tiptoe to lord it over people less powerful than he, that man will not find God wrapped in swaddling clothes and lying in a manger. In our time, he worships sexual fads, or his image in a false mirror, or the all-providing State, or the Progress of History, or what he is pleased to call Science, or some combination thereof; and he must, even for his hideout's sake, make a loud noise about it, lest he hear the "still small voice" that Elijah heard on the mountain of God (1 Kg. 19:12).

And yet it is fitting that God should so appear. Goodness is diffusive of itself, say the schoolmen.[4] It pours itself out in being. To be is to love: and love raises up the beloved. Man rarely manages to grasp this secret of existence, and as soon as he touches it, it slips through his fingers again, and he returns to the big and the overbearing. "God is love," says Saint John (1 Jn. 4:8), not merely *that* God loves, or that God is that pleasant feeling you have for someone you find agreeable. That going-forth from the self to the other, that self-humbling, if I may speak so of God, is not just rewarded by greatness. It is the condition of greatness itself. So when Jesus says, "Whosoever exalteth himself shall be abased; and he that humbleth himself shall be exalted" (Lk. 14:11), he is urging upon us the essence of what it is to be. It is the secret that even Plato did not

---

4   See, for example, Thomas Aquinas, *Summa theologiae*, I, qu. 5, art. 4.

grasp, as he had taken for granted that to love is to need rather than to give away. Man is taller when he bows, as Chesterton said, and that is because every being is greater by love. But man will not see it. Man is too big for love, and too small for glory. Man is also too small for love, and too big for glory.

11

He came unto his own, and his own received him not.

My people, what have I done to you? How have I offended you? Answer me!

I led you out of Egypt, from slavery to freedom, but you led your Saviour to the cross.[1]

THIS VERSE ECHOES THE ONE BEFORE, BUT WITH a new and amplified motif. It is bad enough that the world should not know the Son of God. It is worse when his own people do not receive him.

Before I get to this rejection, I wish to comment upon two of the Greek words here. First, *received*; rendered, plausibly, as *accepted*, in the New American Bible. Whether we think of receiving or accepting, the English must obscure an important echo in the Greek. We have more braiding here, because the verb for *received*, Greek *parelabon*, plays upon the important verb *katelaben*, in the clause, "and the darkness *comprehended* it not." It is now the fourth time that John has pointedly said that something was *not*, and in three of the cases there is profound moral, epistemological, and ontological import. The darkness did *not* seize upon the light, grasp it, enclose it front and back, comprehend it; the world did *not* know the Word, that world that makes itself ignorant by pretending to knowledge of good and evil on its own terms; and now the Word comes among *his own* — the New American Bible has, awkwardly, *what was his own* — and they do not take hold of him, they do not bring him into their minds and hearts.

"For I have *received* of the Lord that which also I delivered unto you," says Saint Paul to the church at Corinth, "that the Lord Jesus the same night in which he was betrayed took bread: And when he had given thanks, he brake it, and said, Take, eat: this is my body" (1 Cor. 11:23–24; Greek

---

1 From the *Reproaches* for Good Friday.

parelabon). Here, to *receive* is to hear, to heed, to take into oneself. So too Paul warns the Thessalonians not to follow the immorality of any man among them "that walketh disorderly, and not after the tradition which he *received* of us" (2 Th. 3 : 6; *parelabosan*). The darkness could not smother the Word; but mankind can shrug it away. That power has God given to us. Love is not love unless it is freely given; and the good that I might be compelled to do against my will does not make me one whit the greater. Says the Father in *Paradise Lost*, foreseeing man's fall:

> Not free, what proof could they have given sincere
> Of true allegiance, constant Faith or Love,
> Where only what they needs must do, appeared,
> Not what they would? what praise could they receive?
>
> (3.103 – 6)

The Word should have been received, taken hold of with gratitude and love, because he came *unto his own*. The Greek is *ta idia*, a neuter plural, here gesturing toward a broad variety of things: the entire nation of Israel, its land, its laws, its history, and its worship. *Idios* with its forms is a demonstrative pronoun that we do not have in English. We might say, "This house of mine," and not simply "my house," to stress that the house belongs to me in a particularly profound way. So did the Greeks use *idios*: the thing named is somehow part of the possessor's *identity*. But the Lord's own people, the people who from the time of their father Abraham had been singled out among the nations to receive his law, those very people did with Jesus what they did with the prophets, and with every other person who dared to tell them they wrought evil. Yet they will dare to say, "We be Abraham's seed, and were never in bondage to any man" (Jn. 8:33). The irony strikes to the heart of their ancient heritage. "Your father Abraham rejoiced to see my day: and he saw it, and was glad," says Jesus, with that manifold vision of time so characteristic of him, looking back upon someone in the distant past who was looking upon someone in the distant future, and seeing that bygone foreseer in the eternally present providence of God (8:56). Jesus then draws the only conceivable conclusion, "Before Abraham was, I AM," uttering the very name of God that only the high priest was permitted to utter, once a year, in the Holy of Holies, on the day of atonement (8:58). But Christ is our "high priest, who is set on the right hand of the throne of the Majesty in the heavens" (Heb. 8:1), and the day of atonement was and is and shall be forevermore that Friday we call Good, when Christ our paschal victim was sacrificed.

"Blow, blow, thou winter wind," goes the sad and sweet song in Shakespeare's *As You Like It*, "Thou art not so unkind / As man's ingratitude." "Ingrate," says the Father in *Paradise Lost*, "he had of me / All he could have" (3.97 – 98). King Lear cries out to the elements on the stormy heath, bidding them to lay bare the cause "that makes ungrateful man." "My people," we portray the crucified Christ as crying out in the Reproaches, those traditional antiphons for Good Friday, "what have I done to you? How have I grieved you? Answer me. I opened the sea before you, and you opened my side with a lance." George Herbert's "The Sacrifice" is a long and tremendously moving expansion of the Reproaches, ever revealing, as a probe retracts the flesh to lay bare an infection, the bitter irony of how man has rewarded his Savior. Here is a representative stanza:

> Betwixt two thieves I spend my utmost breath,
> As he that for some robbery suffereth.
> Alas! what have I stolen from you? Death:
> Was ever grief like mine? (229 – 32)

Gratitude is the virtue whereby the receiver of a gift participates in the generosity of the giver. The gift is free, and the thanks are free, and by "free" I mean more than that these things are uncompelled. They are free in an active and creative sense: they bespeak a soul that is free with itself, ready to give, flowing forth. Praise is the purest expression of gratitude, because then the gift is no third object but the very existence of the one whom we praise. It is the fundamental affirmation, as Josef Pieper puts it: "How good it is that you exist!" Not for your use, not for what you provide, but merely *that you are*: that is why we praise someone when we are at our most innocent and free.

By contrast, how sly, wary, and sparing of praise are the Jews who reject first John and then Jesus! They cannot be satisfied. They will not be satisfied. So Jesus remarks, observing how standoffish they are, and impossible to please:

> But whereunto shall I liken this generation? It is like unto children
> sitting in the markets, and calling unto their fellows,
>   And saying, We have piped unto you, and ye have not danced;
> we have mourned unto you, and ye have not lamented.
>   For John came neither eating nor drinking, and they say, He
> hath a devil.

He came unto his own, and his own received him not.

> The Son of man came eating and drinking, and they say, Behold a man gluttonous, and a winebibber, a friend of publicans and sinners. But wisdom is justified of her children. (Mt. 11:16–19)

Man can always find a reason to fail to do what is good, and to remain ignorant. Praise sticks in his throat.

When Jesus cleanses the Temple, the leaders do not confess that it was something they should have done long before. They ask him for his credentials: "What sign shewest thou unto us, seeing that thou doest these things?" (Jn. 2:18). When he returns to his homeland in Galilee, his countrymen do not turn to him in humility. They behave as if they knew all about him already, leading him to observe that "a prophet hath no honor in his own country" (4:44). When he heals the paralytic at the pool of Bethesda — that is, of *Beth-chesed*, the House of Mercy — the leaders of the Jews do not recall the words of the mighty psalm, *Hodu le-Adonai ki tov, ki le-'olam chasdo*, "Give thanks to the Lord for he is good, for his mercy endures forever" (Ps. 116:1). They grumble that it was the Sabbath, and they "sought to slay him" (Jn. 5:16). When Jesus heals the man born blind, they threaten the man with persecution, and they fall back upon the only lawgiver they acknowledge: "We are Moses' disciples" (Jn. 9:28), for virtuous men prefer to live under the law, which they can understand and which they believe they can fulfill, rather than under grace, which demands the free gift of a loving heart in return.

12

But as many as received him, to them gave he power to become the sons of God . . .

But as I raved and grew more fierce and wild,
At every word
Methoughts I heard one calling, Child:
And I replied, My Lord.[1]

THE GREEK WORD THAT JOHN USES HERE, translated as "sons," is *tekna, children*, without distinction of sex. It is one of four words in the New Testament that are so rendered into English. The others are the diminutive *teknia, little children*, a word that John often uses with touching affection: "And now, little children, abide in him" (1 Jn. 2:28); *paidia, children*, with the possible extension, *servants*, also to be found in John's writings, as when the risen Jesus asks the disciples on the shore of the Sea of Tiberias, "Children, have ye any meat?" (Jn. 21:5); and *hyioi, sons*, sometimes specifically masculine, and sometimes inclusive of both sexes, as in the powerful phrase *sons of God*: "You are all the sons of God by faith in Christ Jesus" (Gal. 3:26; translation mine).

Words for child and children, in every language I know about, imply a hierarchy of obedience, and so it happens that the words may do double duty and refer to someone whose charge it is to obey. *Teknon* simply meant child in Greek, and usually a small child at that — hence the neuter gender, as we in English sometimes and without any trace of contempt refer to a baby as "it." *Teknon* is also, by the way, a distant cousin of Old English *thegn*, the origin of modern English *thane*, the subordinate warrior of a chieftain or prince: Macbeth is the Thane of Glamis and the Earl of Cawdor, but that is not good enough for his ambition. *Pais* meant *child, boy*, but with a sense that he was ready to learn things: hence the *paidagogos, teacher of boys*, or

---

1 From George Herbert, "The Collar" (33–36).

sometimes the servant who went along with the boy to make sure he went to school and did not play hooky. In common parlance *pais* might refer to a servant of any age. For example, the centurion begs Jesus on behalf of his *servant*, lying home sick of the palsy (Mt. 8:6; *pais*). We too in English have *houseboy* to denote, without necessary disparagement or reference to age, a man who cooks and cleans, the masculine equivalent of *housemaid*.

In the Old Testament, we find the phrase *the children of Israel* hundreds of times. It is a generic term, *benai-Yisroel*, literally *the sons of Israel* (Hebrew *ben* = *son*, in the plural potentially including daughters). What we find hardly ever is the phrase *children of God*. "Ye are the children of the Lord your God," says Moses to the people, warning them against certain funeral practices of their pagan neighbors (Dt. 14:1). The psalmist Asaph speaks for God, warning the mighty of the earth, who are figuratively divine, against injustice: "I have said, Ye are gods; and all of you are children of the most High. But ye shall die like men" (Ps. 82:6−7). Just as rare is the phrase *son of God*. We find it in Genesis, where it is mysterious and suspicious, for it came to pass that "the sons of God," whether kings or worse is not specified, "saw that the daughters of men were fair; and they took them wives of all which they chose" (Gen. 6:2), "fair Atheists," as Milton calls them (*Paradise Lost* 11.625). The wicked results of those marriages prompt God to bring the great flood. *Son of God* is implied in a psalm that is crucial to the argument of the writer to the Hebrews, and to Paul when he preaches to the Jews in Pisidian Antioch: "The Lord hath said unto me: Thou art my Son; this day have I begotten thee" (Ps. 2:7; cf. Acts 13:33, Heb. 5:5). *Son of God* can refer to an angel, as when Nebuchadnezzar looks into the fiery furnace and sees the three young men walking about unhurt, "and the form of the fourth is like the Son of God" (Dan. 3:25; late Hebrew *bar*, as in *Simon bar-Jona*, Simon the son of Jonah, Mt. 16:17).

Therefore when Jesus says, "Blessed are the peacemakers: for they shall be called the *children* of God" (Mt. 5:9; Greek *hyioi*, *sons*), he is using a term that would have struck his Jewish hearers as strange and powerful and full of mystery. We are too accustomed to it. The pagans had a veritable rabble of gods and goddesses that bedded down with human creatures all the time. Aeneas, the mythological founder of the Roman people, is addressed as *nate dea*, *goddess-borne*, because Venus had fallen in love with his father Anchises, and she had borne to him a son. The Hebrew scriptures are notable for their desert-scoured and clean lack of any such sexual dabblings of God with women. Hesiod wrote his *Theogony* on the generation of the gods, a theogony which comes to its consummation in Zeus the politician. Zeus suppressed most of his divine ancestors and their kin, uniting his own generation of gods by the exercise of his cunning and will, and then expressing his authority by sheer prolific action — for when Zeus has intercourse with a woman, she is sure to grow with child on the instant. There is, as I have said, nothing of such stuff in the Old Testament. All the "begats" are on the human side, as in "the book of the generations of Adam" (Gen. 5:1).

What, then, does it mean to be a child of God, a son of God? We have seen that even a *figurative* understanding of the phrase is foreign to the Old Testament. That instance in Deuteronomy from the lips of Moses is ironic in its force. It does not affirm so much as it denies — it denies that our ancestors are to be our gods. That is what happens in systems of pagan ancestor worship: in Rome, for example, where your long-dead grandfathers and uncles became the tutelary gods of home and hearth, and you take their figurines or busts made from their death-masks out of a chest to honor them on special days.

There is an easy way out. We can pretend to answer the question by appealing to the figurative. We are children of God if we manage, more or less, to follow the teachings of Jesus, to love one another, to be merciful, to give to the United Way, and so forth. Such a reading, with sugar, can go down the modern throat with ease; as can other figurative exsanguinations of Scripture. The thoroughly modern reader is suspicious of poetry because it threatens to usher us into a realm of being that resists comfortable analysis. But as soon as Jesus makes a specific claim, that supposedly hardheaded fellow puts on his poetry raincoat and raises his poetry umbrella, so that not one drop of what Jesus literally says will touch him. Jesus did not really mean that he was the bread from heaven. He did not really mean that we are to be baptized with water and the Holy Spirit. He did not really mean a score of things that the people about him did not understand. So that all Jesus needed to do to make sure that the Jewish leaders would not persecute him and his followers, was to say, "I was merely using figures of speech," and they would have shrugged and gone their way, knowing that there is often no accounting for poets.

So we often wish to think, making light of everything in our way — of the stark realities that Jesus insists upon, of how deeply he disturbed both the people who wanted to believe in him and the people who did not. We make light of poets too — for poets are usually far more sensitive to the stubborn physical stuff of life than we are. Let us not do so. We should instead assume that John uses the phrase *children of God* to express a full reality, and not just an idea, and that if we are to be those children of God, there must be a generation, a real one, again, and not just an idea.

Here, as so often, we find a deep harmony, despite their far different styles and personalities, between Saint John and Saint Paul, for Paul too is at pains to affirm the real sonship of those who believe in Christ Jesus:

> But when the fullness of the time was come, God sent forth his Son, made of a woman, made under the law,
>
>   To redeem them that were under the law, that we might receive the adoption as sons.
>
>   And because ye are sons, God hath sent forth the Spirit of his Son into your hearts, crying, Abba, Father.
>
>   Wherefore thou art no more a servant, but a son; and if a son, then an heir of God through Christ. (Gal. 4:4–7)

The word here for *adoption*, Greek *hyiothesia*, may well be Paul's own coinage. It means *son-causing, son-making, son-doing, son-establishing*.

What, finally, does it mean that we have the *power* to become — or to be *begotten* (Greek *genesthai*) — the children of God? The two Greek words in the New Testament that correspond to the translation *power* are *dynamis* and *exousia*. When the angel Gabriel tells Mary that she will be with child, and she asks how that can be, since she knows not man, he says that "the Holy Ghost shall come upon thee, and the *power* of the Highest shall overshadow thee" (Lk. 1:35). That is the *dynamis hypsistou*, in Hebrew the *koach-'elion*, the *power of the Most High*, power as *potency, strength, ability* to bring something about. You might think that to be the word of power to top all words of power, but that is not so. We must not confine ourselves to the *efficient* power that tends to be what people in a world of backhoes, computers, railroad trains, derricks, and lasers will think of first and last, the power of one thing touching another thing. There is the power that is inherent to the office or to the very *being* of the one who possesses it. I have mentioned it already. It is power as *authority*, and it is the power denoted here by the Greek *exousia*, power that comes *forth from being*. Jesus says that the Father loves him, because he is willing to lay down his life, and take it up again: "No man taketh it from me, but I lay it down of myself. I have *power* to lay it down, and I have *power* to take it again. This commandment have I received of my Father" (Jn. 10:17–18; *exousian*). "All *power* is given unto me in heaven and in earth"

(Mt. 28:18), says the risen Lord, as he commissions his disciples to go forth and preach to all nations.

We still recognize this sort of power, as when we say that the president of the United States, who does not have the power (*dynamis*) to make the Brooklyn Bridge float in the air, has the power (*exousia*) to pardon a criminal and set him free. But we suppose that the latter power is a matter of mere human consent. That is, we recognize authority only in a limited sense. Authority is delegated, and so it may be withdrawn. We with the thin and envious souls of democrats have a great deal more trouble acknowledging authority as real, not attributed, and as inherent to the person in authority, sometimes by virtue of a real and immutable relation between him and us. Thus does the father in the family, as Saint Paul recognizes, possess a real and not just a culturally constructed authority in the home. The question is not whether the authority is his, but how he will exercise it. From what I can see, most men would like to exercise that authority by ignoring it, but ignoring a mountain does not make it go away.

In point of fact, the writers of the New Testament saw no clean distinction between *dynamis* and *exousia*, and in this regard they were like most people at most times, and not like us. But consider: the priest *can* consecrate the bread so that it becomes the Body of Christ. He has the power (*dynamis*) because God has granted him the *right* to do so (*exousia*). The miracle really happens. If I, who am not a consecrated priest, and who do not possess the authority, say the words of consecration over the bread and wine, nothing happens. I do not have the power. We must not assume that the authority is ours to confer upon ourselves, or that God, like the figurehead of a constitutional monarchy, will sign into law whatever we may please. The Church, says Pope John Paul II, does not have the authority (*exousia*) to make women into priests, and therefore she does not have the power (*dynamis*). Any pretense of doing so will be a sham. The bread and wine will remain bread and wine. From this truth that power flows from authority, and authority is God's to confer, all kinds of corollaries follow *a fortiori*. For one, the Church has neither the authority nor the effectual power to invert God's creation and make it so that a man *can* marry another man. It is an impossibility.

But in Christ we are given the *power inherent to our substantial being* to be begotten as children of God. That will require not the inversion of creation, but its cleansing, renewal, and exaltation, as we will see.

...who believed in his name.

> I bind unto myself the Name,
>> The strong Name of the Trinity;
> By invocation of the same,
>> The Three in One, and One in Three.
> Of whom all nature hath creation;
>> Eternal Father, Spirit, Word:
> Praise to the Lord of my salvation,
>> Salvation is of Christ the Lord. [2]

JOHN NOW RESUMES TWO OF HIS EARLIER MOTIFS, *belief* and *name*. Again, I note how poor and thin the New American Bible translation is. Here it buries the important noun *name* in a participle: "A man named John was sent by God," instead of "There was a man sent by God, whose name was John." The *name* is of tremendous significance. We saw as much when Adam named the creatures in Genesis, in his first act of intellect and God-like rule, "and whatsoever Adam called every living creature, that was the name thereof" (Gen. 2:19). God promises to Abram more than a great lot of descendants: "I will bless thee, and make thy name great; and thou shalt be a blessing" (Gen. 12:2). When God reveals to Moses the name that is not a name, or the name beyond names, because it affirms no mere characteristic but existence itself, "I AM," adding that he is "the God of Abraham, the God of Isaac, and the God of Jacob," he says, "This is my name for ever, and this is my memorial unto all generations" (Ex. 3:15). The name is holy, because he whom it names is holy: "Thou shalt not take the name of the Lord thy God in vain" (Ex. 20:7). Indeed, Jews will refer to God by the phrase *Ha-shem*, *The Name*, and instead of uttering the holy Name in Scripture, they will substitute for it the word *Adonai*, Lord.

A name was not thought to be a mere pattern of sounds, arbitrary, easy to change, and without inherent meaning. Scripture records many dozens of acts of naming, to memorialize a great act of God, or to capture something essential about the place or the person named. So did Abraham name the place atop Mount Moriah, where the Lord stayed his hand as he

---

2   Saint Patrick (372–466), *Atomruig indiu*; trans. Cecil Frances Alexander, 1889.

was about to sacrifice his son Isaac. The Lord provided an unblemished ram instead, and Abraham, remembering ironically what he had said to the boy when he asked his father what was going to be the sheep for the sacrifice, called the place Yahweh-yireh: The Lord shall see (Gen. 22:14). Indeed the psalmists and the prophets are ever speaking about the name of God: "I will praise the Lord [Yahweh, the holy and unutterable name] according to his righteousness: and will sing praise to the name of the Lord most high [Yahweh-'elyon]." "I do not this for your sakes, O house of Israel," says God to the faithless men of the north, "but for mine holy name's sake, which ye have profaned among the heathen" (Ez. 36:22).

In this light do we consider the *name* of Jesus. For by his atoning death and his resurrection, says Saint Paul, "God also hath highly exalted him, and given him a name which is above every name" (Phil. 2:9), a claim that to Jewish ears is equivalent to saying exactly what Paul says, "Jesus Christ is Lord" (2:11). And Saint Peter, challenged by the Jews to tell by what power or name he has been healing and preaching, replies that it is the "name of Jesus Christ of Nazareth, whom ye have crucified," nor "is there salvation in any other: for there is none other name under heaven given among men, whereby we must be saved" (Acts 4:10, 12). James tells his people that they should anoint their sick "with oil in the name of the Lord" (Jas. 5:14). The writer to the Hebrews says that Christ "hath by inheritance obtained a more excellent name" than any of the angels, Christ being the "Son, whom [God] hath appointed heir of all things, by whom also he made the worlds" (Heb. 1:2, 4). John, for his part, focuses on names constantly, insistently. Those who reject Christ condemn themselves, because they have "not believed in the name of the only begotten Son of God" (3:18). We keep God's commandments — think of the Ten Speakings, given to Moses — if we "believe on the name of his Son Jesus Christ, and love one another" (1 Jn. 3:23). In the Apocalypse, names are most urgent matters: Alpha and Omega (Rev. 1:8), the Amen (3:13), Abaddon and Apollyon (9:11), Satan (12:9), Babylon (14:8), Armageddon (16:16), Faithful and True (19:11), the Word of God (19:13), King of Kings and Lord of Lords (19:16), Gog and Magog (20:8), the bright and morning star (22:16). Those who are saved will bear the name of the Lamb upon their foreheads (22:4), and their names will be written in the book of life (21:27).

What, then, is this name? Let us look at the three names by which we know him in Scripture: *Emmanuel, Jesus, Christ.*

First, Hebrew 'Immanu-el. The El is God, common in Hebrew names:

Elimelech means God is king; Eleazar means God has helped; Eliab means God is father. The 'immanu is made up of two parts, the preposition 'im and the pronominal suffix [-a]nu. In Hebrew, prepositions take suffixes to denote an object that is a pronoun, and this suffix denotes the first-person plural, English us. The idea that God is with us is common in Scripture: "The Lord God in the midst of thee is mighty" (Zep. 3:17). I cannot, however, find the exact word 'immanu-el anywhere but in Isaiah, and in the gospel of Matthew. The text of Isaiah is well known: "Behold, a virgin shall conceive, and bear a son, and shall call his name Immanuel" (7:14; Hebrew shemo 'immanu El). Matthew believes that the verse from Isaiah has been fulfilled by the birth of Jesus (1:23). He can believe such a thing only if he affirms from the outset that Jesus is in fact God, God-with-us, as Saint Paul says, "manifest in the flesh" (1 Tim. 3:16).

The Hebrew 'im seems stronger than our English word with. Matthew translates Emmanuel, for those of his readers who do not know Hebrew, as Meth' hemon ho Theos: we might say, God among us, God in our midst. Emmanuel names the reality in one way. The name Jesus names it in another. It is the Hebrew name Yehoshu'a, rendered into English as Joshua, and into Greek as Iesous. That name also is composed of two elements. The first, Yehu, is a contraction of the sacred name of God, and the second is the imperfect of the verb yasha', to save, to set free. The latter is one of the most important verbs in the Old Testament. The whole means either God has saved or God shall save or, with a slightly different sense, God has set free or God shall set free. That is the way the Hebrew verbs are. The ambiguity of time is richly significant, because with the birth of Jesus, God has already set us free, and he shall set us free.

Many of the Church Fathers found great significance in the correspondence between Jesus and Joshua, the judge who assumed his authority from Moses, and who led the children of Israel across the Jordan into the Promised Land. Moses could not bring the people to the end. The Ark of the Covenant was "brought in with Jesus," that is, with Joshua (Acts 7:45). That first Joshua was a foreshadowing of Jesus. The law takes us to the edge of salvation. It does not cross the river. And to be on the near side of the river is to be a thousand miles away.

God shall save — but what does it mean, to save? Greek sozein appears to have the same range of significations as Latin salvare, from which, through the French of the Normans who ruled England after William the Conqueror, we derive our verb save: to be preserved, kept alive, delivered, made *whole.* We are divided against ourselves, in a state of civil war. "For the good that I would I do not," says Saint Paul, "but the evil which I would not, that I do" (Rom. 7:19). Who will deny it? So Milton describes what Adam and Eve are like after the disillusionment of the apple:

> Not only Tears
> Rained at their Eyes, but high Winds worse within
> Began to rise, high Passions, Anger, Hate,
> Mistrust, Suspicion, Discord, and shook sore
> Their inward state of Mind, calm Region once
> And full of Peace, now tossed and turbulent:
> For Understanding ruled not, and the Will
> Heard not her lore, both in subjection now
> To sensual Appetite, who from beneath
> Usurping over sovran Reason claimed
> Superior sway.[3]

Do we want to be made whole? Not when our will is with the usurping appetites, whether for lust, or hate, or vengeance, or ambition. Then we are the traitors against ourselves, and we plant the standards of the enemy in our own hearts. Freedom is frightening to the man who has grown used to his bonds. The very sight of vigorous health makes the weak nerves tremble. C. S. Lewis shows us as much in *The Great Divorce.* "Do you want me to kill it?" says the angel to a man with the lizard of sexual wickedness perched on his shoulder, whispering obscenities into his ear. The man knows that to kill the lizard will be like tearing his heart out — he believes it will kill him too, and in a sense he is right about that. It requires all the man can muster, not by strength of will, but rather, if I may coin a phrase, strength of surrender, so that he finally cries out, "Damn and blast you! Go on, can't you? Get it over. Do what you like . . . God help me. God help me." And the angel crushes the lizard in his fist. The man dies, but rises again, "an immense man, naked, not much smaller than the Angel." The lizard too is transformed, into, says the narrator, "the greatest stallion I have ever seen, silvery white but with mane and tail of gold." Such are the passions when they are governed by man the rider, man, newborn, afire, and whole.

I shall defer until later my discussion of the name, *Christ.*

---

3   *Paradise Lost,* 9.1121–31.

13

Which were born, not of blood, nor of the will of the flesh, nor of the will of man, but of God.

Breathe on me, Breath of God,
Fill me with life anew,
That I may love what thou dost love,
And do what thou wouldst do. [1]

JOHN IS AFIRE WITH POETIC INSPIRATION NOW, introducing several motifs, weaving them together in the braided form we have seen before, and returning, at the climax of the sentence, to two motifs of the greatest significance, the one in contrast with the other: *man* and God.

The New American Bible translators, allergic to poetry, render the sentence in the form of a coroner's report: "Who were born not by natural generation nor by human choice nor by a man's decision but of God." The dreadful result has John saying the same thing twice, in "human choice" and "a man's decision." What is the difference? It is like saying that not only did a man not choose it, he also did not decide upon it — so there. The verse, one of the most powerful and suggestive in all of Scripture, collapses into a sentence characterized by abstraction and redundancy, and all the meanings of *blood*, *flesh*, *will*, and *man*, and all their echoes throughout the Old Testament and the New, are smothered. What was their grudge against John that they should treat him so poorly?

Let us take the motifs one by one. First, *born*. Our English word is the past participle of the verb *bear*, meaning *to carry*, and so it refers principally to what the woman does: she carries a child, until it no longer needs to be carried. We do sometimes use the verb in a figurative sense that brings it closer to the verb *beget*, as when a man might say that his writing a book on

---

1   Edwin Hatch, 1878.

the prologue of the gospel of John was *born of* — that is, *begotten by* — his desire to set down his thoughts on the most influential paragraph in the history of man. But in both Greek and Hebrew, the *bear-beget* distinction does not apply. The Hebrew verb *yalad* means both; and a *yeled* is a boy, a lad, while a *yaldah* is a girl, and *yalduth* means *childhood, youth*. We should keep in mind these suggestions of the fresh and young. Jesus will say to Nicodemus, "Except a man be born again, he cannot see the kingdom of God," and Nicodemus replies, "How can a man be born when he is old? Can he enter the second time into his mother's womb, and be born?" (Jn. 3:3–4). Nicodemus is no fool. He is struggling to understand words that are neither merely literal *nor merely figurative*: and that struggle continues throughout the gospel, as when Jesus's own disciples try to understand what he means by his saying that his flesh is true food. How can a man be born when he is old? That is the crucial question of conversion. Saint Paul urges the people of Ephesus to "put off . . . the old man, which is corrupt according to the deceitful lusts . . . and put on the new man, which after God is created in righteousness and true holiness" (Eph. 4:22, 24). We cannot do that on our own. It must be done to us, in us, and for us, by Christ: "Our old man is crucified with him, that the body of sin might be destroyed" (Rom. 6:6). Only in this way can we fulfill the words of Jesus, who says that we must become like little children; and with what a spirit of youth does the elder John write to the people he has made new in the waters of baptism: "My little children, let us not love in word, neither in tongue; but in deed and in truth" (1 Jn. 3:17).

The Greek for *born* is *egennethesan*, which is the final and climactic word of John's sentence. The parallels do not come across in English, but we have seen forms of this verb already, in *egeneto* (*were made, came to be, came to pass*) and *genesthai* (*to become*), in verses 3, 6, 10, and 12. We might then construe the passages closely, one in light of the other, allowing the senses to cross: All things were begotten by the Word; the world itself was so begotten; and all who believe in his name *come into existence* by God. Again, we must resist the temptation to read with our modern pedestrian sense that places the modifier *mere* before *poetry*. "If any man be in Christ," says Saint Paul, "he is a new creature: old things are passed away; behold, all things *are become* new" (2 Cor. 5:17; Greek *gegonen*; cf. Rev. 21:5). Paul does not say that he is *like* a new creature. Creation itself has begun anew. What the Lord promises in the Apocalypse, a new heaven and a new earth, begins in Christ and by Christ within everyone who is so born.

What about *blood*? It is a word that we feel with every pulse of the heart. We can watch the blood move in our veins. Shall it be obliterated with the ugly phrase, "human generation"? Let us consider this. What is the first mention of *blood* in Scripture? We may say it is in the first of man's holocausts to Satan, when Cain slays his brother Abel, and God says to him, "The voice of thy brother's blood crieth unto me from the ground" (Gen. 4:10). Blood will call upon blood: "Whoso sheddeth man's blood," says God to Noah, "by man shall his blood be shed: for in the image of God made he man" (Gen. 9:6). The Hebrews splashed ram's blood upon the posts and lintels of their doors, so that the avenging angel would pass them by as he slew the first-born of Egypt (Ex. 12:13), and from that time to the time of Christ, sacrifices of blood were made, for "without shedding of blood is no remission" of sin (Heb. 9:22). Of what avail was all that blood? At the best and holiest it was but the foreshadowing, the type, of the blood of the true and only Passover Lamb, as John the Baptist, but a few verses from where we are now, will proclaim: "Behold the Lamb of God, which taketh away the sin of the world" (Jn. 1:29). In the veins of Jesus, says the Baptist, runs the blood of the Lamb who belongs to God and not to the people, the Lamb not for an age and a generation, but forever and for the world. "This cup is the new testament in my blood," says Jesus (1 Cor. 11:25). The very angels triumph over Satan in Christ's blood: "They overcame him by the blood of the Lamb" (Rev. 12:11). It is blood to dye, in grain, the banners of eternal life.

The blood of Christ is strong indeed, but our *flesh* is weak. In Scripture, *flesh* is nearly always a rendering of Hebrew *basar*, from a verbal root having to do with being rosy and fresh, and of Greek *sarx* (cf. English *sarcoma*, coined from Greek). Its meaning includes not just the skin, but the muscles too, as in German *Fleisch = meat*. Sometimes, flesh implies a deep intimacy, as when Adam, beholding Eve for the first time, cries out, "This is now bone of my bones, and flesh of my flesh" (Gen. 2:23). Sometimes it is the general word for man and other living creatures: "The end of all flesh is come before me," says God, when he beholds the wickedness of man, and determines to send the great flood (Gen. 6:13). The flesh yields to the temptations of the flesh, and yet, says the psalmist, God forgave the children of Israel "for he remembered that they were but flesh, a wind that passeth away, and cometh not again" (Ps. 78:39). In the great messianic prophecy of Isaiah, which John the Baptist sees himself as fulfilling, a voice commands the prophet to cry out, "All flesh is grass, and all the goodliness thereof is as the flower of the field" (Is. 40:6). Surely Jesus has that verse in mind when he says, "Consider the lilies of the field, how they grow," clothed by God in glory one day, but no more than "the grass of the field, which today is, and tomorrow is cast into the oven" (Mt. 6:28, 30). We are more than that grass, but we are also like that grass in our weakness and our mutability. To be born again is to be raised from grass to glory indeed. Saint Peter, remembering the words of Jesus and Isaiah and the letters of Paul, says that Christians are "born again, not of corruptible seed, but of incorruptible, by the word of God, which liveth and abideth for ever. For all flesh is as grass, and all the glory of man as the flower of grass. The grass withereth, and the flower thereof falleth away: But the word of the Lord endureth for ever. And this is the word which by the gospel is preached unto you" (1 Pt. 2:23 – 25).

The progression from *blood* to *flesh* continues to *man*, in the Greek genitive *andros*, specifically referring to an adult man, masculine (cf. English *androgen*, a *man-making* hormone). Greek *anthropos* is to Greek *aner* roughly as Hebrew *'adam* is to Hebrew *'ish*. In both languages, the former term is the generic, and means *mankind* in general, or *man* as opposed to God, or angels, or other creatures: "Lord, thou preservest man and beast" (Ps. 36:6; Hebrew *'adam*). "What profit hath a man of all his labors?" asks the Preacher (Ec. 1:3; *'adam*). But in both languages, too, the generic term is grammatically masculine, and can refer loosely to an adult male, when the masculinity of the person is not to the point: "What man among you," says Jesus, "having an hundred sheep, if he lose one of them, doth not leave the ninety and nine in the wilderness, and go after that which is lost, until he find it?" (Lk. 15:4). The Greek there is *anthropos*, *man*, and it seems obvious that although Jesus is not talking about a woman carrying a sheep on her shoulders, the manliness in the man carrying the sheep is not relevant. He continues with the parable of the prodigal son: "A certain man had two sons" (Lk. 15:11). That too is Greek *anthropos*, and we know that the man was a man and not a woman, because he is the boy's father. In Hebrew, it appears that *'ish* can sometimes do the duty of the generic *'adam*: "What is man [Hebrew *'enosh*, man as mortal] that thou art mindful of him? and the son of man [Hebrew *'ish*], that thou visitest him?" (Ps. 8:4).

If John wishes to stress the masculinity of the imagined human being by whose will Christians are *not begotten*, that seems but fitting. For we are not to trust in the might of men. I think here of monumental statuary,

84

everywhere to be found in the ancient world: of Augustus Caesar, for example, wearing his leather breastplate and extending his right arm forth in command. "Look on my works, ye mighty, and despair," sneers the inscription on the pedestal of the ruined colossus of the pharaoh Rameses the Great, as Shelly imagines in "Ozymandias." Or think of Herod, the Idumaean pretender, mighty and craven at once, who "slew all the children that were in Bethlehem and in all the coasts thereof," thinking to catch the Messiah in his deadly net (Mt. 2:16). Jesus is, I believe, markedly masculine, indeed a pattern of strong, determined, virtuous manhood, and for that very reason he has nothing in common with the swaggerers, the overbearing, and the violent among his sex. We might heed the words of Isaiah: "Even the youths shall faint and be weary, and the young men shall utterly fall" (40:30). The passage from boyhood to manhood, for the Jewish lad, meant not that he put on muscle mass, but that he was to enter fully into the word of God. Among Jews now, it means that he becomes a *bar-mitzvah*, a *son of the commandment.*

What, now, does John mean by including the word *will* in his sentence, twice? It is Greek *thelema*, the verbal noun for *thelein, to be willing, to will, to purpose, to determine.* We in English make do with our word *will*, which sometimes denotes the mere future, but which also denotes *willingness*, as when we ask, "Will anyone here do this job?" We are not asking about a future state of affairs; we are asking whether anyone present is *willing* or *wants* to do the job. The Greek word is a crucial one for John, because what it signifies was so important for the Lord: "I came down from heaven," says Jesus, "not to do mine own *will*, but the *will* of him that sent me" (Jn. 6:38). When we pray, says Jesus, we are to say, "Thy *will* be done" (Lk. 11:2). In the garden of Gethsemane, Jesus, bearing the terrible burden of ages of human wickedness, prayed that he might be spared the cup he must drink, but "not my *will*, but thine be done" (Lk. 22:42). In each case it is the same word, Greek *thelema.*

The flesh has its will, and a man has his will, but those who are born again do not depend upon what those wills desire. Freedom is not to will what one chooses, but to will what God chooses, because to obey God is to obey the creator who freely gives and who accepts in return the free gift of man's love. When Jesus tells the Pharisees that the truth shall make them free, they reply by calling upon their lineage — their blood — and their political status — the wills of men: "We be Abraham's seed, and were never in bondage to any man" (Jn. 8:33). But Jesus says that "whoever committeth sin is the servant of sin" (8:34; Greek *doulos, slave*), and there-fore we must decide not *whether* we will obey, but *whom.* The independent man is a fiction. Saint Paul says the same: "Ye were the servants of sin, but ye have obeyed from the heart that form of doctrine which was delivered you. Being then made free from sin, ye became servants of righteousness" (Rom. 6:17–18). That deliverance is ours through Christ, in Christ. We cannot will it on our own. We can surrender to it by grace.

What, after all, do we possess that is really ours? "The sense of own-ership in general," writes Uncle Screwtape to his nephew Wormwood, "is always to be encouraged."[2] Our bodies themselves are not our own to dispense with as we please. "It is as if a royal child whom his father has placed, for love's sake, in titular command of some great province, under the real rule of wise counsellors, should come to fancy he really owns the cities, the forests, and the corn, in the same way as he owns the bricks on the nursery floor." But we become our own by obedience to God rather than to ourselves, or the things we imagine to be ourselves when they are really only the phantasms of mass entertainment, the flitting images of what everybody else is saying and doing, or the suggestions of devils. "When He talks of their losing their selves," says the demonic Uncle, "He only means abandoning the clamor of self-will; once they have done that, He really gives them back all their personality, and boasts (I am afraid, sincerely) that when they are wholly His they will be more themselves than ever."[3]

---

2 C. S. Lewis, *The Screwtape Letters,* ch. xxi.
3 Ibid., ch. xiii.

14

And the Word was made flesh, and dwelt among us.

The Word now dwells among us,
Made flesh, yet very God:
And cherubim sing anthems
To shepherds all abroad.[1]

AT THESE WORDS, IN THE OLD CATHOLIC LIT-
urgy, all the congregation was to genuflect, in a moment of
silence. If there is one sentence that sums up the Christian faith,
it is this one.

Silence, in awe before this miracle of love, a greater wonder than that
which brought the whole physical cosmos into being.

Edward Gibbon, in *The Decline and Fall of the Roman Empire*, was no warm
friend of the Christian faith that swept through the Roman world and
made it new. Yet even he understood that an apparently tiny distinction
in theology and its expression can make all the difference in the world.
The Arian controversy was about whether Christ was, as the orthodox
bishops said, of one *same* being with the Father (Greek *homoousios*), or
whether he was, as the Arian bishops said, merely *similar to* the Father
(Greek *homoiousios*). "The Greek word," says Gibbon, "which was chosen
to express this mysterious resemblance bears so close an affinity to the
orthodox symbol, that the profane of every age have derided the furious
contests which the difference of a single diphthong excited between the
Homoousians and the Homoiousians."[2] Gibbon, an unbeliever, conceded
that more than a diphthong might be at stake, because "it frequently
happens that the sounds and characters which approach the nearest to
each other accidentally represent the most opposite ideas."

What is the distance between God and what is only *like* God? It is an

---

1   Saint Germanus (634–734), *Mega kai paradoxon thauma.*
2   Ch. 21, "The Arian Controversy."

infinite chasm in being. Why, we ourselves would shy away in suspicion from a creature that was not a man, but only *like* one, nor would we settle for something *like* love, when love is what we want.

If we translated John's sentence back into Hebrew, it would read something like this: *Way-yehi ha-dabar le-basar, way-yishkin 'immanu.* The ten words in English are heard as five in Hebrew, five mighty blocks of meaning. First, *yehi*: the imperfect form of the verb *to be, become*; and we can hear in it that echo of the name of God Himself, I AM. Then *dabar, word*: as I have said, the *speaking, acting by speech*; all things pass away, but God speaks, and it is forever. Then the humble *basar, flesh*. Do we hear the reversal? Says the poet Hopkins, thinking of the resurrection:

> Flesh fade, and mortal trash
> fall to the residuary worm; world's wildfire, leave but ash. [3]

Man will hardly take one tentative step down the stairs of social prestige, and that is why, when Jesus says that he among us who would be greatest must become as the least, we immediately look to the safety of allegory, because surely the Lord cannot possibly mean that we should be less than we are. But the Son of God has gone before us, crossing the abysm all the way from the fullness of being to our slight fantastical puff-paste of flesh — flesh that is prone to hunger and thirst, and susceptible to death from the bite of a poor worm. We should stress each of John's words, with insistent force: It happened, it was, from the being of God himself, that the Word, no less than the Word that was face to face with God, and was God, became flesh, no more than flesh.

I cannot presume here to exhaust the significance of those words. That would be like trying to concentrate the whole of Christian history, Christian arts and letters, Christian institutions, Christian prayer, and the Christian understanding of man and God into one little chapter. What does it mean, that the Word became flesh? See the paintings of Giotto, dwelling with loving precision upon the human features of the child Jesus. See the agony stamped upon the face of the dead Christ, painted in dramatic foreshortening by Andrea Mantegna. See the hand of Christ, immensely patient, guiding the finger of a fleshly Thomas into the wound in his side, so that the apostle's fingertip can be seen to bulge below the flap of Jesus's flesh; and that is by Caravaggio, who knew well the weakness and the perversity of the flesh. See Dante, gazing upon the rainbow-like radiance

---

3 "On Nature as a Heraclitean fire, and of the comfort of the Resurrection," 19–20.

of the second Person of the Trinity, suddenly finding that it is "tinted with the figure of a man" (*Paradiso* 33). Or I think of my good old pastor, proceeding into church for midnight Mass on Christmas Eve, holding up from beneath the folds of his cloak the figure of the Christ child, for our adoration. And I hear the strains of a hundred carols:

> Veiled in flesh the Godhead see;
> Hail, the incarnate Deity,
> Pleased as man with men to dwell,
> Jesus, our Emmanuel!

Why, that we have images of God at all is owing to Christ, whose descent among us raised flesh to a glory it never knew. So said Saint John of Damascus, and he and his fellow monks and the common people of the Byzantine empire thus saved for the world what has been more than a thousand years of art and prayer before images of Christ. Against the Muslims and the image-smashers among the Emperor and his counselors at the Byzantine court, he defended the painting of icons as giving honor to the incarnate Word:

> I worship him clothed in the flesh, not as if it were a garment or
> He constituted a fourth person of the Trinity — God forbid. That
> flesh is divine, and endures after its assumption. Human nature was
> not lost in the Godhead, but just as the Word made flesh remained
> the Word, so flesh became the Word remaining flesh. . . . Therefore
> I venture to draw an image of the invisible God. [4]

Our contemporaries do not write hymns about the ultimate answer to the question, "Who is this Jesus of Nazareth?" But it was the central question for the first Christians. So Ignatius, bishop of Antioch, writes to the Ephesians: "There is only one physician — of flesh yet spiritual, born yet unbegotten, God incarnate, genuine life in the midst of death, sprung from Mary as well as God, first subject to suffering then beyond it — Jesus Christ our Lord" (7:2).

Then that flesh dwelt *among* us: Hebrew '*immanu* again, as in the name '*Immanu-el*. John is thinking of Isaiah and of the gospel of Matthew (1:23). The Greek here is *eskenosen en hemon*, from the verb *skenein*, to set a *skene* or roof above yourself, an awning, a shade, a tent: hence the good and earthy translation, *pitched his tent among us*. Such are the *skenas* that Peter offers to pitch for Jesus, Moses, and Elijah on the mount of Transfiguration

---

4 *Treatise on Images*, part one.

(Lk. 9:33). Saint Paul worked for a living as a *skenopoios, a tent-maker*. The Douay translation of Peter's offer, "Let us make three tabernacles," comes from the Latin *tabernaculum*, a small *taberna, a tent*. It is all to the better if *tabernacle* recalls to our ears the liturgical and the sacred, since John with his *skene* appears to be punning — and here I must acknowledge a debt to the New American Bible annotators — on the Hebrew *shekinah*, the *tent* where the power of God *dwells* among the people.

The entire epistle to the Hebrews is implied in this verb, *eskenosen*. It is both tender and astonishing. Man is apt to cast God in *his* image, that is, in the image of someone who wishes to be great so that, like the builders of Babel, he can lord it over his neighbors. The last thing that man expects is that God would come to dwell in his midst not in power but in weakness, even the tender weakness of an infant. The Word at whose utterance worlds came into being is now silent, speechless — what the Latin *infans* means. So we sing in the carol:

> Why lies he in such mean estate,
> Where ox and ass are feeding?
> Good Christian, fear; for sinners here
> The silent Word is pleading. [5]

If it is argued that such a thing is inconceivable, I must instead insist that if we truly understand what it means that an all-benevolent God would condescend to give existence to what has none, then this ultimate condescension of the Word is poetically just and is possible only by God and in God. The redemption is a re-creation, as Saint Paul says, again and again. It is, as I have said, a more radical creation than the first. In the first creation, heaven and earth come into being from the inanity of what was waste and void. In the second creation, Christ comes to dwell within the soul of a creature who, though made in the image of God, has turned with a will toward non-existence. In the first, there is life where there had been nothing. In the second, there is life where there had been death, the will to death. Says Herbert, in the person of the suffering Christ:

> Lo, here I hang, charged with a world of sin,
> The greater world o' the two; for that came in
> By words, but this by sorrow I must win:
> Was ever grief like mine? [6]

---

5   William Chatterton Dix, "What Child is This?," 1865.
6   "The Sacrifice," 205–8.

Or we may turn for insight to a remarkable poem by Robert Browning, "An Epistle of Karshish." Karshish is a traveling physician and philosopher who happens to be combing for remedies and medical wisdom through the inauspicious and backward land of Judea. There he hears of the story of a man raised from the dead by a healer whom the people misunderstood, as laymen are wont to do. So they sentenced their doctor to death. Karshish pretends to believe that that was all there was to it, a doctor condemned by the ignorant, but he cannot drive from his mind the possibility that there was infinitely more. That is because he meets and speaks to that same Lazarus, whom Jesus raised. Lazarus is no great man, no mover and shaker of worldly things. A simpleton, so he seems, unconcerned with war and politics, but then he does not seem so simple, either. What other people consider small matters of piety or immorality cut him to the quick. Karshish does not know what to make of him. Or he does know, and he is hesitant to breathe it aloud. If Lazarus is right in what he says about this healer, then nothing on earth can be the same again. So Karshish ends his letter to his old teacher Abib with these words:

> The very God! think, Abib; dost thou think?
> So, the All-Great, were the All-Loving too —
> So, through the thunder comes a human voice
> Saying, "O heart I made, a heart beats here!
> Face, my hands fashioned, see it in myself!
> Thou hast no power nor mayst conceive of mine,
> But love I gave thee, with myself to love,
> And thou must love me who have died for thee!"
> The madman saith He said so: it is strange.

Or Uncle Screwtape again, imagining what it was like for the man whose sudden death in an air-raid snatched him from the tempters and saved him forever:

> He saw Him. This animal, this thing begotten in a bed, could look
> on Him. What is blinding, suffocating fire to you, is now cool light
> to him, is clarity itself, and wears the form of a Man. [7]

Or as a later poet has imagined the blind Bartimaeus healed by the hands of Jesus: "Lord, I was blind, and now I see your face."

---

7 C. S. Lewis, *The Screwtape Letters*, ch. xxxi.

And we beheld his glory, the glory as of the only begotten of the Father ...

O wondrous type! O vision fair
Of glory that the Church may share,
Which Christ upon the mountain shows,
Where brighter than the sun he glows.[8]

THE NEW AMERICAN BIBLE TRANSLATORS, never missing a chance to paint in gray, put *saw* in place of *beheld*. And in some languages, that is what you must settle for. Luther's German has *wir sahen*, we saw, and Jerome's Latin has *vidimus*, same thing. But the Greek verb here, a passive derivative of *theorein* (cf. English *theory*), is not the ordinary verb for seeing. The verb *theorein* is rather rare in the New Testament. It has to do not with a casual vision, even if the sight is remarkable, as when you are walking down a street and you see a car swerve off the road and hit a tree. It has to do with a determined kind of seeing, a steady and deliberate gaze, as in contemplation or amazement, as when Jesus utters the mighty words: "I *beheld* Satan as lightning fall from heaven" (Lk. 10:18; Greek *etheoroun*).

Think of the difference between *seeing* and *beholding*. My dog can see. Even a blind man can see, in a figurative sense. He may say, "I see," meaning, "I understand." But only a rational being can *behold*, because only a rational being can hold the object of his vision at a distance, to look upon it, to enter into its beauty or terror or grandeur. Think of an artist standing back from his painting, to see it as much with his mind and heart as with his eyes. Seeing may be a mere physical action. Beholding *must be an intellectual action*, and you can behold without understanding what you behold. Indeed, if you understood fully the object of your gaze, I might say that you could behold it no more. For you it would be a dead thing, pinned to the wall of facticity.

At this point someone may object that we no longer use the word *behold* in ordinary speech, so we should not use it in a translation of the Bible.

---

8 *Caelestis formam gloria*, 15th c., trans. John Mason Neale, 1854.

That objection is foolish. Let me try to explain why, because Christian congregations seem these days to believe that there is something special about the demotic.

The objection assumes that Jesus and the people he preached to and the evangelists who spread the good news were as indifferent to poetry as we are. But in this regard, as I have tried to show, we are the bizarre ones, the outliers. Every human culture but our own has had its characteristic poetry, beloved by ordinary people and passed down from one generation to the next. And indeed Jesus often preached in poetic form, so that his words might strike the heart more powerfully, and the mind might retain them more readily and surely. The objection also assumes a linguistic monotone, a single register for all human enterprises. But again, we are projecting our unusual dullness upon others. Because all human cultures have their poetry, all human languages have a range of registers, including the poetic and the sacred. A man does not pray in the same words he uses to buy a mule. A man does not court a woman in the same words he uses to buy a mule, or at least he has not been known to do so in the past. When Jesus and his apostles prayed and sang hymns at the Last Supper, it was probably in Hebrew, the old sacred language from which their everyday Aramaic had derived. If they sang a Hebrew psalm, the Hebrew they sang was not like the prosaic Hebrew of the historical books, such as the Chronicles. Some Hebrew words that we find in the psalms or in the poetry of the prophets we find there and there alone. So, for the translator, it is more precise, more faithful to the original, not less, to search for a poetic word that conveys a special meaning, rather than to settle for an ordinary word that misses both the meaning and the emotional and sacral force.

We *beheld his glory*, says John. I have commented already on the Hebrew word that John has in mind here: *chabod, glory*, from a root that suggests *weight, substance*. The Greek *doxa* is different. It has to do with an *appearance* that is so mighty and so clear, it bears incontrovertible witness to its own truth. Our current word *glory* comes, through the Norman French, from Latin *gloria*, suggesting fame, pomp, and splendor. Its Christian sense has taken the word by storm, and has lifted it up; in Latin outside of the Christian scriptures it might suggest boasting, as in the stock *miles gloriosus, the swaggering soldier* of pagan Roman comedies. A touch of that sense remains in the old translations of Saint Paul writing about boasting: "But he that glorieth, let him *glory* in the Lord" (2 Cor. 10:17; Greek *kauchomai, to boast*; a completely different verb, not related to *doxa*). We in Old English had a fine old noun for glory, *wuldor*; the cowherd-turned-poet Caedmon calls the creation *weorc Wuldorfaeder, work of the Glory-Father*.

If we could hear a song of light, *glory* would be the word for it. So Dante begins his *Paradiso* with the splendid line, *La gloria di colui che tutto muove*; here it is in English, with the lines that follow and complete the thought:

> The glory of the One who moves all things
>   penetrates the universe with light,
>   more radiant in one part and elsewhere less:
> I have been in that heaven He makes most bright,
>   and seen things neither mind can hold nor tongue
>   utter, when one descends from that great height,
> For as we near the One for whom we long,
>   our intellects so plunge into the deep,
>   memory cannot follow where we go.
> Nevertheless what small part I can keep
>   of that holy kingdom treasured in my heart
>   shall now become the matter of my song.

"Not unto us, O Lord," sings the psalmist, "not unto us, but unto thy name give glory" (Ps. 115:1). But through the mercy and love of Christ, we are granted the great promise, to enter into the splendor of God. That splendor is veiled no longer, for the veil has been taken away, says Saint Paul: "We all, with open face beholding as in a glass the glory of the Lord, are changed into the same image from glory to glory" (2 Cor. 3:18). The glory changes the soul that beholds it in love.

Dogs may fawn and cringe, but men and angels give glory, and by God's gift they participate in that glory, "for in their looks divine," says Milton of the innocent Adam and Eve, when Satan beholds them for the first time, "the glorious image of their Maker shone."[9] By sin we have lost that original glory, but in the resurrection even our flesh will be radiant: "It is sown in corruption; it is raised in glory" (1 Cor. 15:43). What is beyond glory — beyond the glory of God? Nothing; and that is why so many of our old hymns end with a stanza of *doxology*, a *glory-speech*, usually in honor of the Trinity; that is why every psalm recited in the Divine Office ends with a doxology; and it is why we have doxologies in all the letters of the New Testament. John records a poetic prayer of Jesus that is all about the giving and returning of glory, from Father to Son and from Son to Father, and from both in the Spirit to those who know

---

9 *Paradise Lost*, 4. 291–92.

them. It is an extended doxology, beginning with these words, "Father, the hour is come; glorify thy Son, that thy Son also may glorify thee" (Jn. 17:1). The Apocalypse, a book conscious of its being not just last in a series but ultimate in ascent, is full of doxologies, beginning with this one that seems to concentrate into several verses many of the main motifs of the whole book and of the gospel of John:

> John to the seven churches which are in Asia: Grace be unto you, and peace, from him which is, and which was, and which is to come; and from the seven Spirits which are before his throne;
> And from Jesus Christ, who is the faithful witness, and the first begotten of the dead, and the prince of the kings of the earth. Unto him that loved us, and washed us from our sins in his own blood,
> And hath made us kings and priests unto God and his Father; to him be glory and dominion for ever and ever. Amen. (Rev. 1:4 – 6)

To return to the gospel prologue: John, dancing again with his motifs, repeats the accusative *doxan* to describe what manner of glory he intends. It is the *glory as of the only begotten of the Father: doxan hos monogenous para patros.* The New American Bible translators flatten the participle, and tuck the powerful noun, Father, which ends the clause with great emphasis, into a possessive adjective: *the glory as of the Father's only Son.* When we think of *begetting,* we think of a son or a daughter, but when we think of a son or a daughter, we do not necessarily think of begetting. The participle here is important. It is meant to echo that verse from the psalm that was central to the thoughts of the evangelists and apostolic writers concerning Christ: "Thou art my Son; this day have I begotten thee" (Ps. 2:7). It repeats the verb that we have seen above, *genesthai, to come to be, to be made, to be begotten.* The unusual use of *monos,* only, as a prefix highlights a motif that is crucial for the New Testament: "To God only wise, be glory through Jesus Christ for ever. Amen" (Rom. 16:27); "who only hath immortality, dwelling in the light which no man can approach unto" (1 Tim. 6:16); "to the only wise God our Savior, be glory and majesty" (Jude 25); and, of course, the *only begotten Son.*[10]

We may say that all sin is a denial of the exclusive rights and duties implied by *only.* "[God] *alone* shall you serve," says Jesus, rebuffing Satan the tempter (Mt. 3:10). The spouses in a wedding pledge to cleave *only* to one another. The murderer takes a human life whose disposition belongs to God and to no other. John will draw a clear line to separate those who are

---

10 See Jn. 1:14, 1:18, 3:16, 3:18, Heb. 11:17, 1 Jn. 4:9.

of God from those who are not: they alone come from God who confess that Jesus Christ has come among us in the flesh (1 Jn. 4:2).

The Son implies the Father, the begetter. If it is not impious to say so, I believe that God may have withheld from the children of Israel his being their Father, lest they fall into the nature-worship common among their neighbors, with its attribution of potent sexual action to the gods and goddesses. We have some slight evidence that they considered God to be, metaphorically, a father: the names Joab and Abiah mean "The Lord is a father," and Eliab, "My God is a father." And the psalmist says that God is "a father of the fatherless" (Ps. 68:5), describing his merciful providence, and "as a father pitieth his children, so the Lord pitieth them that fear him" (Ps. 103:13). Such attributions are rare, however, and they name not what or who God is but some characteristics of what he does.

But it may be the single most salient feature of the preaching of Jesus, that he calls God "Father," and permits or rather commands everyone to do the same. Thus we are to be chary of having people see us give alms, so that the "Father which seeth in secret himself" shall reward us (Mt. 6:4). And we are not to concern ourselves overmuch with what we are to eat or drink or wear, for "your Father knoweth that ye have need of these things" (Lk. 12:30). We are to be as bold as children before a loving Father, praying, "Our Father which art in heaven, hallowed be thy name" (Mt. 6:9). Jesus does not say that God is like a father, but that he is the Father: it is not a metaphor but a name.

It is profoundly personal. For Jesus does not only call God a Father or even the Father, but my Father and, simply, Father. How can he do such a thing? Let us not reduce Jesus to a religious revolutionary. The world has seen plenty of those. When Jesus uses the name, Father, he reveals something about himself, about God, and about the relationship of the Father and the Son. Again, I think that Saint John has captured those moments when the Lord spoke privately and intimately to small gatherings of people, or to his closest friends alone, for references to the Father, in John's gospel, in his letters, and in the Apocalypse outnumber such references in all the other New Testament books taken together — and those other references are many indeed. Jesus can call God Father not because he knows something about God, but because he knows God, simply, immediately.

But even that is not an adequate description of their relationship. Jesus knows the Father in a way that Moses and Elias not only did not know the Father, but could never know him. "All things are delivered unto me of my

Father: and no man knoweth the Son, but the Father; neither knoweth any man the Father, save the Son, and he to whomsoever the Son will reveal him" (Mt. 11:27). We are not talking about degrees of proximity or friendship, but about a new thing revealed to man, the wondrous inner life of God who is a communion of Persons: "I and my Father are one," says Jesus (Jn. 10:30). "Hear, O Israel, the Lord our God is one Lord," cry the Jews in the great prayer of their faith (cf. Mk. 12:29, Dt. 6:4); and therefore we must love the Lord with all — not some, but all — our heart and soul and mind and strength. The oneness of God demands, from us, singleness and fullness of worship. But when Jesus says, if I may render it back into Hebrew, *'Ani w'abi echad*, ending on that most powerful word, *echad*, one, he is taking that prayer and bursting it open. He affirms *both* the unicity of God, and his own *unity* — not just a fine harmony, not just agreement — with the Father. Then to love God is to take part in the love which God Himself is.

We should be clear about what that means. C. S. Lewis says, in *Mere Christianity*, that the Christian statement that "God is love" (cf. 1 Jn. 4:16) makes no sense outside of the doctrine that there is more than one Person in the Godhead:

> If God was a single person, then before the world was made, He was not love. Of course, what these people mean when they say that God is love is often something quite different: they really mean "Love is God." They really mean that our feelings of love, however and wherever they arise, and whatever results they produce, are to be treated with great respect. Perhaps they are: but that is something quite different from what Christians mean by the statement "God is love." They believe that the living, dynamic activity of love has been going on in God for ever and has created everything else.[11]

One word more about the name, Father. It is not Parent. Try to think of your "parent." You cannot do it. You must straightaway concentrate your attention on either your mother as your mother or your father as your father. That is wholly natural. We have tried to scrub out the deep reality of sex, turning the world and even our fellow men into one vast neuter flatland. That was not possible in Hebrew. Verbs in Hebrew have masculine or feminine gender, according to the gender of the subject. Every verb in the Old Testament that has God as an agent is in the masculine gender. Jesus does not advise us to call God "Father, sort of," or "Parent of

11 From "Beyond Personality: First Steps in the Doctrine of the Trinity," ch. 4.

indiscriminate gender." I do not pretend to be wiser than Jesus. I cannot say of myself, "The Father and I are one." I will submit to be taught. It is not, finally, that God is like a father, but that human fathers are rather shadowy manifestations of the fatherhood of God. We are fathers, figuratively, by comparison with God's fully actualized fatherhood, from whom all *fatherhood* in heaven and on earth derives its name (cf. Eph. 3:15; Greek *patria*).

... full of grace and truth.

> The God whose will by moon and sun
> And all things in due course is done,
> Is borne upon a Maiden's breast,
> By fullest heavenly grace possessed.[12]

PERICHORETIC NARRATIVE, AGAIN; JOHN NOW names in Greek the *grace* he has hinted at, for those of his readers or listeners who were Jewish, in his own name and the name of the Baptist, *Yochanan*. He also resumes the motif of *truth*, which will be one of the great themes of his gospel. See for example the mighty and climactic verse of testimony, when blood and water come forth from the pierced side of the Lord: "And he that saw it bare record, and his record is true: and he knoweth that he saith true, that ye might believe" (Jn. 19:35). Saint Augustine is not the only Church father who will often call Jesus by the name, Truth. For when Truth himself speaks, what poor sinner of a man should gainsay him?

John has also introduced a new motif, in the simple adjective *full*. It is another word of power. "The world is filled with the grandeur of God," says the poet Hopkins. In the beginning, God blessed the lowly creatures of the air and the sea, saying, "Be fruitful, and multiply, and fill the waters in the seas, and let fowl multiply upon the earth" (Gen. 1:22). "The earth is the Lord's, and the fullness thereof," says the psalmist (Ps. 24:1). "I am who fill / Infinitude," says the Father in *Paradise Lost*, when he is about to create the worlds (7.168 – 69). In the Hebrew mind, fullness was about more than a container's capacity. The verb *mala*, to fill, gives

---

12 Latin, 9th c., *Quem terra, pontus, aethera*, trans. John Mason Neale.

us also the verbal noun *millu'*, *a fulfilling*, in the sense of a *dedication* or *consecration*. So the ram that was sacrificed to elevate Aaron and his sons to the priesthood is the *'eyl ha-millu'im*, the *ram of consecration* or, literally, *the ram of fulfillings*. And Aaron and the sons were not to leave the tent for seven days while they were being made priests, "until the days of your *consecration* be at an end: for seven days shall [God] *consecrate* you" (Lev. 8:33; Hebrew *millu'*, *yemalle'*).

Suppose we think of filling, then, in the sense of the fullness of a holy action, a consecration that requires the completion of a liturgy or a penance enacted in a specified sacred time. That sheds a holy light upon the words of Saint Paul: "When the fullness of the time was come, God sent forth his Son, made of a woman, made under the law" (Gal. 4:4). The time of the law is a time of preparation and anticipation. It is like the days when Aaron was hidden in the tent. It is like the growing fullness of a woman who is with child — in the image the Preacher uses, woman as a full vessel, *meleah* (Ecc. 11:5). The six days of creation attain their fullness, their consecration, in the Sabbath. The whole of the history of Israel attains its fullness, its consecration, in Christ. Jesus himself says so: "The time is fulfilled, and the kingdom of God is at hand; repent ye, and believe the gospel" (Mk. 1:15).

The evangelists are eager to show us at every opportunity that something shadowed forth in the old dispensation is now made full. In Matthew, it is usually a prophecy. "Then was fulfilled," he says, recounting Herod's slaughter of the innocents, "that which was spoken by Jeremy the prophet, saying, In Rama was there a voice heard, lamentation, and weeping, and great mourning" (Mt. 2:17−18; cf. Jer. 31:15). The evangelists do not initiate this look back to see what partial revelations have now been fulfilled. Jesus *begins* his ministry by declaring it: "This day is this scripture fulfilled in your ears," he says to his fellows in the synagogue at Nazareth, referring to the messianic vision of deliverance in Isaiah (Lk. 4:21; cf. Is. 61:1−2). It is the central message of Hebrews: "God, who at sundry times and in divers manners spake in time past unto the fathers by the prophets, Hath in these last days spoken unto us by his Son, whom he hath appointed heir of all things" (Heb. 1:1−2). To return to Saint Paul, the time under the strictures of the law was as childhood, tutelage, and bondage, preparing the way for the grace of Christ, which fulfills the old and raises it to a glory it could not attain on its own:

Even so we, when we were children, were in bondage under the
elements of the world:

But when the fulness of the time was come, God sent forth his
Son, made of a woman, made under the law,

To redeem them that were under the law, that we might receive
the adoption of sons.

And because ye are sons, God hath sent forth the Spirit of his
Son into your hearts, crying, Abba, Father. (Gal. 4:4–7)

You cannot give what you do not have. Whence shall man seek his fulfillment, if not from him who enjoys the fullness of all good? "I am who
fill / Infinitude," says the Father in Milton's poem, as he grants to the Son
the commission to create the world (*Paradise Lost*, 7.168–69). The joy of
the evangelists, and this is especially evident of John, is that they dwell
within the fullness of Christ, and so are filled with him. Jesus longs to
share that fullness. "These things have I spoken unto you," he says to the
apostles, "that my joy might remain in you, and that your joy might be
full" (Jn. 15:11), and, "Hitherto have ye asked nothing in my name: ask,
and ye shall receive, that your joy may be full" (Jn. 16:24). In Jesus is
bounty, such bounty as if he had made of himself one open wound of
love. That is how he makes us full.

The Son of God *made himself empty*, says Saint Paul, leaving his glory
at the side of the Father, to dwell among us in the form of a man, a
slave, becoming obedient unto death (Phl. 2:7). Paul may well have in
mind the Hebrew verb *riyq, to empty, to make empty*, as in *being poured out*:
"Prove me now forthwith," says God in the final messianic prophecy of
the Old Testament, "if I will not open you the windows of heaven, and
pour you out a blessing, that there shall not be room enough to receive
it" (Mal. 3:10). But the Hebrew adjective *reyq*, derived from the root of
the verb, means not just *empty* but *vain, worthless, unprofitable*: "When
you have done all those things which are commanded you," says Jesus
to his disciples, "say, We are unprofitable servants: we have done that
which was our duty to do" (Lk. 17:10). Hence the use of the adjective as
a noun, to describe moral fools, as when Michal sneers at David, after he
danced in a linen apron before the Ark of the Covenant: "How glorious
was the king of Israel today, who uncovered himself today in the eyes
of the handmaids of his servants, as one of *the vain fellows* shamelessly
uncovereth himself!" (2 Sam. 6:20; Hebrew *reyqim*). It is the source of
the Aramaic *raca*, the word Jesus used, preserved in Matthew, when he

says, "Whoever shall say to his brother, Raca, shall be in danger of the council" (Mt. 5:22).

So we should not grow sentimental about this emptying. The Greek adjective *kenos, empty,* is like the Hebrew adjective, in that both also suggest what is of no avail, of no account, futile: hence Saint Paul says, that if we live and walk in the Spirit, we shall "not be desirous of *vain glory*" (Gal. 5:26; Greek *kenodoxoi*), and he warns the Corinthians, who seemed, as dabblers in Greek philosophy might be, to remove the flesh from the Resurrection and spiritualize everything, that "if Christ be not risen, then is our preaching *vain,* and your faith is also *vain*" (1 Cor. 15:14; Greek *kenon, kene*).

I have dwelt so long upon the idea of emptiness or emptying, because without it we cannot grasp what it means to be filled with the blessings of God. This is not the same thing as self-abnegation, for the plain reason that when Christ works in us, we become more truly ourselves than we were before: think of the saints in their sharp individuality. Consider these words from the *Dialogues* of Saint Catherine of Siena:

> Eternal Greatness! You made Yourself low and small to make man great. On whichever side I turn I find nothing but the abyss and fire of Your charity. And can a wretch like me pay back to You the graces and the burning charity that You have shown and show with so much burning love in particular to me beyond common charity, and the love that You show to all Your creatures? No, but You alone, most sweet and amorous Father, are He who will be thankful and grateful for me, that is, that the affection of Your charity itself will render You thanks, because I am she who is not, and if I spoke as being anything of myself, I should be lying by my own head, and should be a lying daughter of the Devil, who is the father of lies, because You alone are He who is. And my being and every further grace that You have bestowed upon me, I have from You, who give them to me through love, and not as my due.

To be *filled with grace* is to be filled with the free bounty of God. But the very essence of a gift is that it must be received as such, and that is why the old masters, when they painted the three Graces, portrayed two of them as facing towards the beholder and one as facing away. The point was to show that there was grace in receiving as in giving. If you want to earn all you get, you will never get much, and what you do get, you may not like.

15

John bare witness of him, and cried, saying, This was he of whom I spake.

THE FORERUNNER NOW ENTERS THE GOSPEL AS a human character, speaking and acting, as the evangelist resumes his name and the motif of *witness*. John the Baptist is also the first dramatic character in the gospel of Mark. In Mark, he foretells the coming of one who is greater than he is. In John, his first words are to say *that he has already foretold* the coming of that greater man. Those critics who say that the gospel of John includes, in the final chapter, an addition by a later hand, because the book does not end where it "should" end, might trouble to notice that the book's narrative does not begin where it "should" begin, either, and that recapitulating habit, as I have said, is characteristic of the vision of time and sequence that John gives us, and which he attributes to the Lord himself. We always seem to be occupying several times at once, such as looking back upon a time (that of John's preaching) when someone else (the Baptist) looked back upon a time further back (that of Isaiah's prophecy) to foretell the coming of someone in a future time (Jesus), which time is now here. For the man whose coming has been foretold says not only that he will fulfill the old prophecies, but that they are already fulfilled in his person, and that they will be fulfilled in glory in a future time that is beyond all future time: in his Father's house.

That makes what Virgil gives us in the *Aeneid* look like a game of tic-tac-toe to a master of chess. Yet Virgil, not John, had by far the greater talent as a writer. John's greatness comes not from himself but from *who Jesus is*.

The Baptist *cried* out (Greek *kekragen*, from *kragozein, to cry, shout*). We think right away of the verse from Isaiah, to which the evangelist John, along with the other evangelists, refers: "I am the voice of one *crying* in the wilderness, Make straight the way of the Lord, as said the prophet Esaias" (Jn. 1:23; cf. Is. 40:3; Greek *boontos*). John has given us the Greek translation of Isaiah exactly as it is in the Septuagint. There, the verb for *crying* is stronger than *kragozein*: Greek *boein, to yell*). The Hebrew verb in Isaiah is *qara*, and it means more than shouting. The English *call* comes close to having the same broad range: to call, as in to give something a name (cf. Gen. 1:5, "And God *called* the light day"), to summon (cf. English, to *call forth*), to proclaim, to invoke (cf. English, to *call upon*), and even to read aloud; it was therefore what Jesus was doing in the synagogue at Nazareth. With such a range in mind we see that the Baptist was doing more than raising his voice in a wilderness. He was proclaiming, declaring; even, though there was no book before his eyes, reading aloud the prophecies of the Messiah to come.

We may set the Baptist's cry alongside — how shall we say it? — our many glimpses into the shyness of the Lord, his silences, and his withdrawal into quiet places. The multitudes follow him, and the more they do, the more he bids them be silent, as Matthew says, so that the prophecy of Isaiah might be fulfilled:

> Behold my servant, whom I have chosen; my beloved, in whom my soul is well pleased: I will put my spirit upon him, and he shall shew judgment to the Gentiles.
>
> He shall not strive, nor cry; neither shall any man hear his voice in the streets.
>
> A bruised reed he shall not break, and smoking flax shall he not quench, till he send forth judgment into victory.
>
> And in his name shall the Gentiles trust. (Mt. 12:18–21; cf. Is. 42:1–4)

A man possessed by a demon, raving in the synagogue itself, cries out when Jesus is near, saying, "What have we to do with thee, Jesus of Nazareth?" But Jesus merely rebukes the devil, saying, "Hold thy peace, and come out of him" (Lk. 4:33–34). The disciples on the stormy Sea of Galilee cry out in the night when they see someone approaching them on the water, believing it to be a spirit, but Jesus simply says, "Be of good cheer; it is I; be not afraid" (Mt. 14:27). The man whose boy was torn by the spirit, flailing on the ground and foaming at the mouth, asks Jesus to heal his son, and when Jesus replies that all things are possible to those who believe, he "cried out, and said with tears, Lord, I believe; help thou mine unbelief" (Mk. 9:24). Finally, at his entry into Jerusalem on the colt of an ass, triumphant and humble at once as only a true king can be, the people cry out, "Blessed be the King that cometh in the name of the Lord: peace in heaven, and glory in the highest." When the Pharisees tell

Jesus to rebuke the people, he replies, "If these should hold their peace, the stones would immediately cry out" (Lk. 19:38 – 40).

Rarely does the Lord raise his voice, but when he does, we should pay attention, because we are the ones who compelled him to do so: "Jesus, when he had *cried* again with a loud voice, yielded up the ghost" (Mt. 27:50; Greek *kraxas*).

He that cometh after me is preferred before me: for he was before me.

THE NEW AMERICAN TRANSLATION HERE HAS two left feet: "The one who is coming after me ranks ahead of me because he existed before me."

In order to avoid referring to Jesus as *he*, the translators thrash about and come up with *the one*. If their reasoning is that in ordinary speech we do not use the locution *he who*, well, we also do not use *the one who*, not in the sense in which they use it here. When we say *the one*, we always imply either *the many* or *the other*: "When you enter the lobby, a pack of reporters will want you to comment. Keep your mouth shut, but walk aside with *the one who* comes from the *Gazette*. He will be wearing a red cap." "The needs of the many outweigh the needs of *the one*." Neither sense is in play in the Baptist's words. It is always awkward, and often a grammatical smash-up, to replace *he* with *the one*.

The translation *ranks ahead of me* ruins the parallelism and the sense of time. When you are *ahead of someone*, you are farther along the same path. That is, you have passed by, and he is only now getting to where you were. But the Greek suggests *priority* in a broad sense: he who comes after me, says John, is *emprosthen mou gegonen, made to be before me*, because *protos mou en*, he was before me. The *emprosthen* / *protos* play on words can only be caught in English by *before* / *before*, thus: Christ is *before* John in one sense (that of being his superior) because he was *before* John in another (that of being, simply). Since John is several months older than Jesus, and since he began his ministry before Jesus began his, he can only mean here something mysterious, something that neither he nor his hearers can fully understand, but that has already been declared in this gospel, when the evangelist says, "In the beginning was the Word."

So when the Baptist's disciples come to him, reporting that Jesus was now baptizing and that everyone was flocking to him, John reminds them, "Ye yourselves bear witness, that I said, I am not the Christ, but that I am *sent* before him" (Jn. 3:28; Greek *apestalmenos*). John is not the bridegroom, but rather the friend of the bridegroom who hears the bridegroom's voice and rejoices, and "this my joy therefore is fulfilled. He must increase, but I must decrease" (Jn. 3:29–30). John echoes another Messianic passage in Isaiah, "unto us a child is born, unto us a son is given," and "of the increase of his government and peace there shall be no end" (Is. 9:6–7). The Hebrew verb for *increase* is *rabah*, and it takes us back to creation itself, when God blessed mankind and said, "Be fruitful, and *multiply*" (Gen. 1:28). We may then hear John as saying, "He must multiply," he must become great, "and I must make myself small," insignificant. For the significance of the Forerunner is that he points to him who comes after him: and in this his purpose is accomplished.

"The function of equality," says C. S. Lewis in his essay, "Membership," "is purely protective. It is medicine, not food." It is "a quantitative term and therefore love often knows nothing of it." It is a prophylactic in the secular state, to guard against evils, "but in the Church we strip off this disguise, we recover our real inequalities, and are thereby refreshed and quickened." Jesus never talks about equality. He talks about love. He never talks about how in the kingdom of Heaven all shall be the same. He says that the first shall be last and the last shall be first. It is with that same reversal of expectations that he evaluates the person and the mission of the Baptist: "Verily I say unto you, Among them that are born of women there hath not risen a greater than John the Baptist: notwithstanding he that is least in the kingdom of heaven is greater than he" (Mt. 11:11).

Consider the surprises here. Moses gave the Law, and the whole of the Pentateuch was attributed to him; but John the Baptist, who never wrote a word, was greater than Moses. David was the greatest of the kings of Israel; but John the Baptist, wearing the skin of a camel and foraging for grasshoppers in the desert, was greater than David. Isaiah the prophet foretold the Messiah, but John the Baptist, who but pointed in the direction of Jesus, was greater than Isaiah. Abraham, the father of a progeny as numberless as the sands on the shore; Aaron, the first high priest and the progenitor of every high priest to come; Solomon, to whom God gave the wisdom of rulership, greater than any ruler ever had — all these, says Jesus, were lesser than the lone crier in the wilderness. For John the Baptist's prophecy was wholly to prepare the people for Jesus and to turn them his way. He was thus greatest in being least, and yet, Jesus goes on to say, the least in the kingdom of heaven is greater than the Baptist is. For the Baptist had not yet suffered his final witness, his martyrdom at the hands of Herod.

16

And of his fullness have all we received and grace for grace.

ORE PERICHORESIS: JOHN RESUMES THE motif of *fullness* from verse 14; the Greek for *we have received, elabomen,* echoes the verbs in verses 5 (*comprehended, katelaben*), 11 (*they received, parelabon*), and 12 (*they received, elabon*); the motif of *grace,* particularly a fullness of grace, echoes verse 14; and the first person plural, in English rendered as the separate pronoun *we,* also returns to verse 14.

It is interesting, this *we.* It presumes the existence of a community, a church, with its birth in Christ and its aim and completion in Christ. Of the other evangelists, Saint Luke also begins with an acknowledgment of this plurality of persons whom Christ has made one, when he says he wishes to set in order those things "as they delivered them unto us, which from the beginning were eyewitnesses, and ministers of the word" (Lk. 1:2). So do the authors of letters to the churches, most notably in the way they name Jesus, bespeaking solidarity with one another, and affection and awe for him: "Our Lord Jesus Christ" (cf. Jude 4). In John, the pronoun assumes an urgency, as it implies not only that John is speaking for the church, but that the church likewise is testifying for John: "This is the disciple which testifieth of these things and wrote these things: and we know that his testimony is true" (Jn. 21:24).

Perhaps the plural is a special revelation for us, as we in the western world are encouraged to affirm a contradiction in terms, namely, the privacy of religion. There can be no such thing, even if we think of it from the human side alone, since man is always and ineluctably a social being. He can no more have a private religion than he can have a private culture, a private society, or a private nation. Religion, culture, society, and nationhood may be many things, but private is not one of them. We can look at it also from the side of the divine. When Jesus is asked which of the commandments is the greatest, he replies thus:

Thou shalt love the Lord thy God will all thy heart, and with all thy soul, and with all thy mind.

This is the first and great commandment.

And the second is like unto it, Thou shalt love thy neighbor as thyself.

On these two commandments hang all the law and the prophets. (Mt. 22:37 – 40)

You cannot love God if you do not love your neighbor. Even those among us who do not believe in God may agree with that, though they would be hard put to tell why they agree with it or whence they have gotten the notion that the one love was related to the other. We might also reverse the order and come up with something that startles: You cannot love your neighbor if you do not love God. And here people will hedge or grow indignant. They will give examples of all kinds of benevolence at the hands of pagans and unbelievers. Benevolence, however, is not what the evangelists mean by love. If it were, Jesus could hardly have said, after he washed the feet of the apostles, "A new commandment I give unto you, That ye love one another; as I have loved you, that ye also love one another" (Jn. 13:34). Benevolence is good advice for getting on in the world. I mean no disrespect for it. Some people are blessed with constitutions that make it easy. Others, not so. But benevolence, as the object of a command? It is not strong enough to bear the force of a command.

Kindliness is no new command. Nor is friendliness, for even a pagan will do a good turn for his friend. Saint Paul did not say that these three remain, faith, hope, and good feelings. The love that he says is everlasting does not come from us. It is a gift to us: the greatest of all gifts, proceeding from the Lord and reaching its fulfillment in seeing him face to face. The *we* that the Christian utters must always have its root in Christ, and its flower and fruit in Christ, lest the Church be reduced to just another human organization, a religious club, a political party. Saint John insists upon this radical orientation to and from Christ as strongly as does Saint Paul, because he heard it from the lips of Jesus himself: "I am the vine, ye are the branches: He that abideth in me, and I in him, the same bringeth forth much fruit: for without me ye can do nothing" (Jn. 15:5). Many a Christian body has degenerated into a human organization, even one actuated by good intentions and strong social feeling, such as the Young Men's Christian Association, which is no longer dedicated to young men, and is no longer Christian. To what extent it remains an *association* in other than name and legal structure is not clear to me. What is clear to me is that it does not take long for Jesus's words to be fulfilled: "If a man abide not in me, he is cast forth as a branch, and is withered; and men gather them, and cast them into the fire, and they are burned" (15:6).

On our own, we can do nothing — we cannot even properly and consistently call ourselves "we." These truths are co-inherent. Man cannot save himself. Man must empty himself in order to be filled with God, so that he may become himself indeed. Man, made not to be alone but to dwell in a life of love for God and neighbor, can form a true communion only by the gift of God. Man must love God with all his heart and soul and mind, and love his neighbor as himself. Man cannot will that love unless God has loved him first and given him the grace of love. As I have said before, Saint Paul and Saint John, so different in their personalities, so strikingly unlike one another in every superficial feature of their writing, are preaching the same Christ.

I might put it this way. Man in his fallen nature is always in danger of losing his grasp upon the first person pronouns. His "I" is often a simulacrum, a piece of play-acting, a disguise, a muddle of fads and fashions in speech, clothing, behavior, and opinion. His "we" is a political caucus, a loose association, a tribe, or a mob. In Christ, he becomes a new creation, and he can say, with Saint Paul, "Not I, but Christ liveth in me" (Gal. 2:20), living for God and for all men, in the "we" of the Church.

We cannot re-create ourselves. We do not make our own Church. That is why John says that we have received from the fullness of Christ "grace for grace," in Greek *charin anti charitos*, with a striking use of the preposition *anti*, to suggest an exchange, grace in exchange for grace, grace for grace, *quid pro quo*. The odd and wonderful thing here is that God does not give us grace in exchange for some act of our own whereby we please him first. It is not an economic barter. The giving is initiated by God, and the giving is never miserly, never with an aim at leading us into a merely economic or quantitatively proportionate response. John is quite clear about this: "Herein is love, not that we loved God, but that he loved us, and sent his Son to be the propitiation for our sins" (1 Jn. 4:10). So also Saint Paul: "But God commendeth his love toward us, in that, while we were yet sinners, Christ died for us" (Rom. 5:8). We saw nothing lovely in our Savior (cf. Is. 53:2), but he saw in us the loveliness that would be ours when he loved us and implanted his love in our hearts. All is grace.

17

for the law was given by Moses...

With Moses and Elijah nigh
The incarnate Lord holds converse high;
And from the cloud, the Holy One
Bears record to the only Son.[1]

WHEN JESUS APPEARED TRANSFIGURED, IN raiment as radiant as the sun, he stood between Moses and Elijah, who were not merely his precursors, but who derived from him as the Word whatever authority they possessed. Moses gave to the children of Israel *the words*, that is, *the commandments* of God, and the Jews believed that Moses himself was the author of the first five books of Scripture, which are still so numbered in German bibles, so that Genesis is the First Book of Moses. We should keep that in mind, because then we may associate also with Moses the mighty words that John has echoed and transcended: "In the beginning God created the heaven and the earth" (Gen. 1:1).

Moses speaks for God. He was the first and the greatest of all the prophets: "And there arose not a prophet since in Israel like unto Moses, whom the Lord knew face to face" (Dt. 34:10). Yet one thing that Jesus does consistently is to place Moses in a subordinate and relative position. When Jesus says, boldly, that divorce is evil, for "what therefore God hath joined together, let not man put asunder" (Mt. 19:6), the Pharisees press him further, asking him why Moses incorporated divorce into the Law. And Jesus replies, "Moses because of the hardness of your hearts suffered you to put away your wives: but from the beginning it was not so" (Mt. 19:8).

Let us think about this carefully. As we have had many an occasion to see, a variety of times are present to Jesus at once. We have "the beginning," Greek *arche* again, and Hebrew *reshith*, referring to the original intentions of God the Creator; and notice that Jesus speaks authoritatively about

---

1 *Caelestis formam gloriae*, 15th c.; trans. John Mason Neale, 1842.

that time in the beginning, as if he were present there. Then we have the time of Moses, which time includes the Pharisees who are speaking to Jesus right now. Moses permitted divorce because of the hardness of your hearts, he says, as if they were among the wayward and stiff-necked people who so often gave Moses cause to grieve. Then we have the time of Jesus, who returns to the beginning. He does so not as a lover of the archaic, for "new wine must be put into new bottles" (Mk. 2:22), but as a redeemer and restorer: "And I say unto you, whoever shall put away his wife, except it be for fornication, and shall marry another, committeth adultery" (Mt. 19:9). That high and holy view of marriage, by the way, is implied by Jesus's miracle at Cana (Jn. 2:1 – 11), his use of the marriage feast as an emblem for the kingdom of God (cf. Mt. 22:1 – 14), his casting himself in the role of bridegroom (cf. Mt. 25:1 – 13, Mk. 2:19 – 20), the Baptist's referring to him as the bridegroom (Jn. 3:29), and the great revelation that the Church herself is the bride of Christ. So says John of the Apocalypse: "And the Spirit and the bride say, Come" (Rev. 22:17).

We see the pattern of going before, above, and beyond Moses throughout the gospels. "Among those that are born of women there is not a greater prophet than John the Baptist," says Jesus, as I have noted above, "but he that is least in the kingdom of God is greater than he" (Lk. 7:28). Or consider one of the several dramas that Saint John brings before us to behold, when Jesus healed the man born blind.

We are in Jerusalem, and Jesus and his disciples pass by the blind man. And they ask him a rabbinical question: "Master, who did sin, this man, or his parents, that he was born blind?" (Jn. 9:2). It is not a foolish question. "I will *greatly multiply* thy sorrow and thy conception," says God to Eve, after she and Adam had sought their good from themselves and from the natural world, not from God; "in sorrow shalt thou bring forth children" (Gen. 3:16). The verb is again *rabah*, *to multiply*, in emphatic form; it had been the verb of blessing, when God said, "Be fruitful, and *multiply*" (Gen. 1:28). We should notice that all of family life is hurt by our proclivity to sin, and that is borne forth in one story in Genesis after another. We might find the consistency oppressive, but that we are so used to it — I mean not in Genesis but in our own lives.

Sin is justly and predictably punished in our most intimate relations, and thus do I understand the formula found four times in the law of Moses: "I the Lord thy God am a jealous God, *visiting the iniquity of the fathers upon the children unto the third and fourth generation* of them that hate me; And shewing mercy unto thousands of them that love me, and keep my commandments" (Ex. 20:5). So then, the disciples of Jesus are attempting to understand the man's blindness in the story of faithless Israel, and, more narrowly, in a putative story of the man's own family life. Jesus does not deny the words of God as revealed to Moses. They are true, in a limited application. But they are not the ultimate truth. The ultimate truth is providential in a way the disciples do not expect, and this new way embraces all of time and, potentially, all human suffering. The man is blind, says Jesus, "that the works of God should be manifest in him" (Jn. 9:3).

From this moment, we are in the realm of new creation. Jesus calls himself "the light of the world," echoing that prime and mysterious creation in the beginning. Then he repeats the work of God in making man. He takes some of the dust of the earth, and he mingles it with his spittle. Think of water here: the initial unmeaning "waters" of creation, whereupon the spirit of God moved, the water of the Jordan that Joshua and the people crossed, the water of the same river that John used to baptize, the water in the jars at Cana, the living water Jesus promises to the woman at the well, the water of Jesus's tears at the tomb of Lazareth, the water with which Jesus washes his disciples' feet, the water that flowed from his pierced side, the voice of the Lord that is "as the sound of many waters" (Rev. 1:15), the crystal sea of the Apocalypse, and the river of life flowing from the side of the Lamb. Think of the grains of dust, the minims of creation, to which we return in death, "for dust thou art," says God to Adam, "and unto dust shalt thou return" (Gen. 4:19). With this mud, then, this paste of dust and water, *his water*, Jesus anoints the eyes of the blind man, and then gives him what appears to be a Mosaic command for the unclean: "Go, wash in the pool of Siloam" (Jn. 9:7). John will not let the command pass without a comment: the pool's name means *sent*, in Greek *apestalmenos*, exactly the same word he used to refer first to the Baptist: "There was a man sent from God," whose name was God is gracious (Jn. 1:5).

Moses was sent, the other prophets were sent, the Baptist was sent, and Christ himself has been sent, and he will send forth his own apostles; and of the sending and being sent there shall be no end, until the final coming of the Son of Man. But the first sendings-forth are shadows of Christ, who sends and is sent. "He went his way therefore," says John, referring to the blind man with powerful simplicity, "and washed, and came seeing" (Jn. 9:7).

The Pharisees hear of it, and they are not pleased, because "it was the sabbath day when Jesus made the clay, and opened [the man's] eyes" (Jn. 9:14). In a similar situation, Jesus will refer to the purpose of the Sabbath, when people ask him a good rabbinical question, "Is it lawful to heal on the sabbath days?" (Mt. 12:11). They are seeking occasion against him. But in this healing of the blind man that we read of in John, Jesus does not settle for the penultimate truth — whether the Sabbath is made for man, or man for the Sabbath. Here creation itself is really at issue, for Jesus, on the sabbath, when "God rested from all his work" (Gen. 2:2), is working, quite deliberately working, for "I must work the works of him that sent me, while it is day" (Jn. 9:4).

When the Pharisees ask the blind man what he thinks of Jesus, the man says the least he could be expected to say: "He is a prophet" (Jn. 9:17). But if this is true, then, given what Jesus did, how he did it, and when he did it, we have a prophet greater than Moses. That is why the Pharisees fall back upon the Law. "We are Moses' disciples," they say to the man, who has showed them some courage in his backtalk. "We know that God spake unto Moses: as for this fellow, we know not from whence he is" (28 – 29). The man in return plays the rabbi to the rabbis, saying, "Since the world began"— notice that he too has the first creation in his gaze —"was it not heard that any man opened the eyes of one that was born blind. If this man were not of God, he could do nothing" (32 – 33). For remember God's first creation: there was nothing but darkness, and then there was light. The teachers know very well that they are now *being taught*, and they do not like it. So, with Moses and the psalmist in mind, they cry out, "Thou wast altogether born in sins, and dost thou teach us?" And they cast him out (34).

We may be tempted to consider their actions as typical for people holding on to privilege and power. They are, but they are more, and the Pharisees themselves and the man born blind know it. A choice must be made. You must remain stolidly in the Law, and in the fallen and unredeemed old creation, or you must turn to grace, and be made new. The Pharisees understand that they are in crisis. Jesus does not leave them the option of a liberal interpretation of the Law. A greater than Solomon, or Jonah, or Jacob, or Elijah, or Moses is here.

...but grace and truth came by Jesus Christ.

O Word of God incarnate,
O Wisdom from on high,
O Truth, unchanged, unchanging,
O Light of our dark sky;
We praise thee for the radiance
That from the hallowed page,
A lantern to our footsteps,
Shines on from age to age. [2]

JOHN RESUMES THE MOTIFS OF GRACE AND TRUTH (Hebrew *chanan, emeth*), and the verb translated as *came* is our friend *egeneto, happened, was made, came to pass, became, came into being.* What is new here, in this strand of the braid? Not the idea of a name. We have seen that, in verses 6 ("whose name was John") and 12 ("who believed in his name"). And I have said that John expects us to think of the names *Jesus* (from the Hebrew, *God shall save*) and *Emmanuel* (Hebrew, *The Lord is in our midst*). Here the name is uttered aloud: Jesus, along with the word that names who he is, the Christ, Greek *Christos*, translating Hebrew *Mashiyach, Anointed One,* from the verb *mashach, to anoint.* It is the word that John transliterates into Greek as *Messias,* twice. Once is when Andrew, the friendly apostle, rushes to get hold of his brother Simon, saying, "We have found the Messias" (Jn. 1:41); the other time is when the Samaritan woman at the well, entering into a conversation with Jesus about the true way to worship God, says, "I know that Messias cometh," and he will be the one to settle the matter (Jn. 4:25). Jesus says, "I that speak to you am he" (26). The way John phrases it in Greek stresses the tremendous claim that Jesus is making. *Ego eimi,* says he, I AM, who speak to you. The stress does not come across in English, because we always use the personal pronoun: we say, "I am," "he is," "we are," and so forth. That is not so in Greek—or in Latin or Italian, for that matter. In those languages, the form of the verb alone tells whether the subject is first or second or third person, singular or plural. The pronoun is unnecessary, so that when you do use it, it is

2 William Walsham How, 1867.

114

deliberate and emphatic. "Sono io, che ti parlo," says Jesus to the woman, in my Italian translation: "I am [he], who speak to you."

So then, every time we see the name Christ, we should think, Messiah, the Anointed One; and every time in the New Testament we find a reference to anointing, we should think of Jesus the Christ.

Why should the ancients have attached so much significance to anointing? A few observations about ordinary life are in order. The civilization of the Mediterranean depended upon grain and the olive. From the olive came the precious oil with which they cooked their food, because there was not nearly enough animal fat to suffice for such a large population, and animal fat goes rancid quickly in a warm climate. The olive itself was nourishing. It provided them light for their lamps, burning steadily, without much smoke. When the Jesuits and Franciscans introduced the olive to California and Mexico and central America, they raised the welfare of the people mightily, even if they had done nothing else — and they did many other good things, too, quite before we get to the sacraments. People in the Mediterranean world even cleaned themselves with oil — they did not make soap — and perfumes were based in oil, not alcohol. Medical treatment required oil: recall that the Good Samaritan had compassion on the man who was left for dead, and "bound up his wounds, pouring in oil and wine" (Lk. 10:34), wine to cleanse the flesh, and fatty oil to stanch the bleeding. The Greeks traded overseas with oil, clay pots full of it. Oil was as important for their economy as petroleum is for some nations now.

We can tell how terrible a fate the widow of Zarephath and her son were waiting for in the long drought and famine, when Elijah asked her for a little bread, and she said, "As the Lord thy God liveth, I have not a cake, but an handful of meal in a barrel, and a little oil in a cruse: and behold, I am gathering two sticks, that I may go in and dress it for me and my son, that we may eat it, and die" (1 Kg. 17:12). But Elijah instructed her to make him a cake first, and then one for herself and her son, and "the barrel of meal shall not waste, neither shall the cruse of oil fail, until the day that the Lord sendeth rain upon the earth" (14). We remember Canaan, the Promised Land, as flowing with milk and honey, but it is also a land rich in the olive. If the children of Israel follow the commandments, says the Lord, "I will give you the rain of your land in his due season, the first rain and the latter rain, that thou mayest gather in thy corn, and thy wine, and thine oil" (Dt. 12:14).

Oil was a constant feature of the pre-sacramental worship under the law of Moses. It was a sign of cleanliness and holiness. On the eighth day after a leper had been declared free of the impurity, he was to make a sacrificial offering that included a pint of oil, which the priest would sprinkle before the Lord, dabbing the man's ear and thumb and toe, and pouring the rest upon the man's head (Lev. 14:10–18). Aaron and his sons were made priests in a ceremony marked by a generous measure of oil. Says the Lord to Moses: "Then thou shalt take the anointing oil, and pour it upon his head, and anoint him" (Ex. 29:7). Unity among brothers, says the psalmist, is "like the precious ointment upon the head, that ran down upon the beard, even Aaron's beard: that went down to the skirts of his garments" (Ps. 133:2). "Thou anointest my head with oil," says David in the loveliest of holy songs (Ps. 23:5). So did the elderly prophet Samuel: "Then Samuel took the horn of oil, and anointed [David] in the midst of his brethren" (1 Sam. 16:13). The prophecy of deliverance that Jesus cited in the synagogue in Nazareth, and applied to himself, fairly declares that he is the Messiah: "The spirit of the Lord God is upon me; because the Lord hath anointed me to preach good tidings to the meek" (Is. 61:1; cf. Lk. 4:18).

Jesus the Christ, the anointed of God, is thus priest, prophet, and king, but not as Aaron was priest, or as Isaiah was prophet, or as David was king. They were the shadows and the forerunners. He is the full reality. As such he confers upon believers a participation in his priesthood, prophetic calling, and kingship. For "ye are a chosen generation," says Saint Peter, in his own role as priest, "a *royal* priesthood, an holy nation, a peculiar people, that ye should show forth the praises of him who hath called you out of darkness into his marvelous light" (1 Pet. 2:9; Greek *basileion*, *kingly*). John combines all three roles in his great paean of thanksgiving to Jesus the Anointed One:

> JOHN to the seven churches which are in Asia: Grace be unto you, and peace, from him which is, and which was, and which is to come; and from the seven Spirits which are before his throne;
> And from Jesus Christ, who is the faithful witness, and the first begotten of the dead and the prince of the kings of the earth. Unto him that loved us, and washed us from our sins in his own blood,
> And hath made us kings and priests unto God and his Father; to him be glory and dominion for ever and ever. Amen. (Rev. 1:4–6)

18

No man hath seen God at any time.

Pleasant are thy courts above
In the land of light and love;
Pleasant are thy courts below
In this land of sin and woe.
O my spirit longs and faints
For the converse of thy saints,
For the brightness of thy face,
For thy fullness, God of grace.[1]

JOHN'S GREEK IS EMPHATIC: *THEON OUDEIS HEO-raken popote*, beginning with the direct object, God, as if to say GOD *no one has seen ever.* It may seem that John here contradicts Isaiah: "In the year that king Uzziah died I saw also the Lord sitting upon a throne, high and lifted up, and his train filled the temple" (Is. 6:1). That was the vision that made Isaiah cry out, "Woe is me! for I am undone, because I am a man of unclean lips, and I dwell in the midst of a people of unclean lips: for mine eyes have seen the King, the Lord of Hosts" (5). The prophet Micaiah said to the wicked King Ahab, using similar words but casting them in the context of an allegorical scene, "Hear thou therefore the word of the Lord: I saw the Lord sitting on his throne, and all the host of heaven standing by him on his right hand and on his left. And the Lord said, Who shall persuade Ahab, that he may go up and fall at Ramoth-gilead?" (1 Kg. 22:19–20). Moses went up the mountain to speak with God, but the people were terrified by the thunder and lightning, and stood far away, "and Moses drew near unto the thick darkness where God was" (Ex. 20:21). This is to see God, in a manner of speaking. It is to see him as distant, dangerous, shrouded in darkness: "Dark with excessive bright thy skirts appear," Milton's angels sing (*Paradise Lost*, 3.380). And yet the same God has made us for communion with him: "When thou saidst, Seek ye my face; my heart said unto thee, Thy face, Lord, will I seek" (Ps. 27:8).

---

1   Henry Francis Lyte, 1834.

Let us then imagine the scene at the Last Supper, a scene of profound solemnity, anticipation, fear, gratitude, and love. Judas has departed to do his evil work. Jesus has announced to the apostles that he will be with them only a little time longer. Peter, always impetuous, speaks up first and says that he will follow wherever Jesus goes, even if it means laying down his life. Jesus then foretells that Peter will deny him three times before the cock crows. But he comforts them again, saying that he goes to prepare a place for them in the Father's house, "and whither I go ye know, and the way ye know" (Jn. 14:4). Thomas, hard-headed and to the point, objects. How can we know the way, he says, when we do not know where you are going? "I am the way, the truth, and the life," says Jesus. "No man cometh unto the Father, but by me. If ye had known me, ye should have known my Father also: and from henceforth ye know him, and have seen him" (6–7). Then Philip says, "Lord, shew us the Father, and it sufficeth us" (8).

Show us the Father. Philip seems to assume that Jesus was speaking metaphorically when he said that anyone who truly knows him knows the Father also. Philip is asking instead for a theophany. He believes that Jesus has the power to reveal to them the Father in all his might and glory, in a vision that would make Isaiah's vision seem like the fleeting memory of a dream. After all, Jesus will say to the high priest at his trial, "Hereafter thou shalt see the Son of man sitting on the right hand of power, and coming in the clouds of heaven" (Mt. 26:64), and Saint Paul encourages the church at Thessalonica with hope for the same theophany: "For the Lord himself shall descend from heaven with a shout, with the voice of the archangel, and with the trump of God" (1 Th. 4:16). But that is not what John means here by seeing the Father, now, and not what Jesus meant when he answered Philip, saying, "Have I been so long time with you, and yet hast thou not known me, Philip? he that hath seen me hath seen the Father; and how sayest thou then, Shew us the Father? Believest thou not that I am in the Father, and the Father in me?" (Jn. 14:9–10). The Greek for *seen* here is the same verb that John has used in our verse, saying that no man has ever seen God.

Jesus is not saying that we get a fair idea of what the Father is like when we pay attention to what he, Jesus, says and does. That would be presumptuous of any man to say, unless some farther condition applies, something that was prophesied exactly and that no one believed. It is that the Father and the Son are one. Not that the Son is the Father, simply. The Son does nothing but what he sees the Father do. The Son obeys the Father. But the obedience of a good son for his wise father is metaphorical, analogical, by comparison with the union of the divine Son and the Father. Jesus says that he is "in the Father" and the Father is in him. The Hebrew would be even more powerful in its terseness: *'ani b'ha-ab w'ha-ab bi*. No closer unity is conceivable in word or thought.

The only begotten Son, which is in the bosom of the Father, he hath declared him.

Behold me then, me for him, life for life
I offer, on me let thine anger fall,
Account me man; I for his sake will leave
Thy bosom, and this glory next to thee
Freely put off, and for him lastly die
Well pleased.[2]

JOHN REPEATS THE MOTIF OF THE *MONOGENOS*, the *only begotten*, and the motif of the *Father*, weaving into his sentence the new word, *bosom*, along with a verb having to do with making a declaration, and an important participle used as a noun—necessarily obscured in the English translation.

To the participle first. John does not simply say, "the only begotten, in the bosom of the Father." He could have done that. He could have used an ordinary verb, thus: "The only begotten, who rests in the bosom of the Father," or "who dwells" or "who is." Instead he says *ho on, who being*. The construction appears awkward, unless you understand that he has gone out of his way to express himself so. He is again thinking of the great revelation to Moses when God spoke from the burning bush. Moses asks God to tell him what he is to say when the children of Israel ask the name of him who sent him. In the Greek Septuagint, God responds thus: *Ego eimi HO ON: I am THE BEING*. "Thus shall you say to the sons of Israel: *THE BEING* has sent me to you" (Ex. 3:14; my translation).

Whenever, in the gospel of John, we hear Jesus saying, "I am he," we should mentally eliminate the predicate nominative, and hear only what

---

2 Milton, *Paradise Lost*, 3.236–41.

the words are in Greek, *ego eimi*, I AM. The assertion of deity is particularly
clear when the Pharisees say that Abraham is before Jesus, that is, before
him and above him in authority, and Jesus replies, "Before Abraham was,
I AM" (8:58). They understand exactly what those words imply, and so
"they took up stones to cast at him" (59).

The word for *bosom*, Greek *kolpos*, is rare in the New Testament. We
find it three times in Luke's gospel. Once is when Jesus says that if we give,
we shall receive far more in return: "Good measure, pressed down, and
shaken together, shall men give into your bosom" (Lk. 6:38). That saying
of Jesus turns into a blessing what had been Asaph's curse: "Render unto
our neighbors sevenfold into their bosom their reproach" (Ps. 79:12). We
can perhaps imagine someone receiving what he has bought in grain by
holding forth his robe at his lap. The other two instances in Luke come
from the moving parable of the rich man and the beggar Lazarus, who after
his death was taken up into the bosom of Abraham (16:22 – 23). There,
Lazarus is as Abraham's beloved son. John uses the word *bosom* one other
time too, at the Last Supper, when "there was leaning on Jesus's bosom one
of his disciples, whom Jesus loved," and Simon Peter motioned to him to
ask Jesus who he meant when he said, "One of you shall betray me" (Jn.
13:21 – 24). John there is referring to himself, as if he were Jesus's son; and
Christian tradition has had it that John was the youngest of the apostles, a
tradition for which there is some indirect evidence, in that John remained at
the foot of the cross with Mary and the other women. The Roman soldiers
would not likely concern themselves with women and a beardless youth.

We have, then, a word that in context expresses the closeness of Father
and Son in a deeply moving and personal way. There is nothing abstract
about the bosom. The Son is not said to be in the bosom of the Father
because he shares his Father's mind. He shares his Father's mind because
he is himself the Being, and the Being in the bosom of the Father, who
is also the Being. The New American Bible translators, evidently skittish
about the meaning of "bosom," have the Son merely "at the Father's side,"
again reducing a noun and a personal name to a possessive adjective,
ruining the emphatic word-order, and blurring the close identification
of the Father with the Son. My associate stands at my side. My son is in
my heart. He dwells in my bosom.

John does more here than say that Jesus, the only-begotten Son of God,
has declared God to us. He implies that *only* Jesus can do that. The root
of the word that John uses, *exegesato*, is the same that gives us the English

derivative *hegemony*, rulership, and suggests a declaration from one who has the authority to make it. The verb is used elsewhere only in the Acts of the Apostles. When Paul had his dramatic encounter with the risen Christ, he began to preach about him in the synagogues of Damascus, causing the Jews to seek his life. So he fled to Jerusalem, where the Christians were understandably wary of embracing the man who had persecuted them, but "Barnabas took him, and brought him to the apostles, and *declared* unto them how he had seen the Lord in the way, and that he had spoken to him, and how he had preached boldly at Damascus in the name of Jesus" (Acts 9:27; Greek *diegesato*). When the angel appeared to the centurion Cornelius and commanded him to seek out Simon Peter, the man called his servants, "and when he had *declared* all these things unto them, he sent them to Joppa" (10:8; Greek *exegesamenos*). And when Paul and Barnabas came to Jerusalem to settle matters between Gentile and Jewish followers of Christ, Peter rose up and said that "God, which knoweth the hearts, bare them witness, giving [the Gentiles] the Holy Ghost, even as he did unto us," and James confirmed Peter's generosity, saying, "Simeon *hath declared* how God at the first did visit the Gentiles, to take out of them a people for his name" (15:14; Greek *exegesato*). "Who shall *declare* his generation?" said the prophet Isaiah, referring to the suffering Servant of God, and Philip explained to the Ethiopian eunuch that the prophecy had been fulfilled in Christ (8:32; cf. Is. 53:7; Greek *diegesetai*).

The point is not just that Jesus has revealed to us something we did not know before. It is that Jesus has *declared it to us*, with the authority of one who knows the truth, and one who in his proper person demands to be heard. Thus does the final verb of our passage return us to the verbal noun we began with: "In the beginning was *the Word*."

I have sometimes met people who say that they do not believe in God because they lack the evidence. They never tell me what evidence they are looking for. And what evidence can there be? If I see a print of a shoe in the mud, I infer that someone wearing a shoe has walked through my yard. It is a sign that one material thing, the shoe, has had an observable effect upon another material thing, the mud. The print functions as a sign because of the specific and finite characteristics of the two objects. Not everything is a shoe, and not everything is mud.

But God is ever in act, wholly, in every cranny of space, in every least flicker of time, in every tiniest bit of matter, in every working of every physical law that he himself has willed into being, so that he is as it were secreted away by being everywhere, rather than sipping some ambrosia upon Mount Olympus. He is also, unlike the Stoic abstraction of a Mind permeating all things as water permeates a sponge, a personal Being. He is not background radiation. How do you come to know a Person? Not by inferring his existence. That can be done without faith, hope, or charity. Satan knows that God exists. "The devils," says Saint James, "also believe, and tremble" (Jas. 2:19).

You come to know a Person by encounter. God is no boor, forcing himself upon us. He would be sought. He gives us both the command to love Him, and the adventure of the quest. He honors us with a world that is wide open. By his nature he is hidden in his own unfathomable depths, and that might cause us to despair, except that he has come to us:

> Begotten of no human will,
> But of the Spirit, thou art still
> The Word of God in flesh arrayed,
> The promised fruit to man displayed. [3]

And he comes in a way that both reveals himself as love, and disarms our pride:

> When came in flesh the incarnate Word,
> The heedless world slept on,
> And only simple shepherds heard
> That God had sent his son. [4]

And that same humble Incarnation continues in the sacrament of the Eucharist:

> O Food of men wayfaring,
> The Bread of Angels sharing,
> O Manna from on high!
> We hunger; Lord, supply us,
> Nor thy delights deny us,
> Whose hearts to thee draw nigh. [5]

If we wish to see the Father, we must turn to Christ who has *declared* him, made him clear to our sight. The call is personal and intimate, and so must the reply be. There is no other way.

---

3 Saint Ambrose, 340-397, *Veni, Redemptor gentium*, trans. John Mason Neale.
4 W. Anchors, 1721.
5 Latin, 7th c., *O esca viatorum*, trans. Athelstan Riley.

Further Considerations

ON STYLE AND THE WOMAN CAUGHT IN ADULTERY

Forensic experts in handwriting can tell a true signature from a forged signature by some tic or habit betrayed by the forger, or by some telltale that suggests that the forger has stopped or slowed down in the middle of writing a single letter in a word. A man's signature is not quite like a fingerprint, but it is close. We are tempted to believe that the same science that can sort out a genuine signature from a forged signature can reliably be applied to authors, even when the texts in question are few and rather short. Let me assure the reader that this is not so.

I have already said that no one would assign The Merry Wives of Windsor and King Lear to the same author, if we did not already know that Shakespeare wrote both plays. And, granting that Shakespeare wrote both, no one would assign them to the same period of his career, if we did not already know the dates they were licensed for performance. Here we are talking about texts that are longer than any of the gospels, and much longer than any of the letters of Saint Paul.

Suppose we had every one of Shakespeare's plays, but suppose their authors were all unknown. Suppose also that we knew that sometimes two or three men would collaborate on a single play. The theories such a condition would engender! Consider the climax of All's Well That Ends Well, when the callow young Bertram is presented with evidence of his having gotten with child not an unmarried woman he tried to seduce, but his own wife Helena, whom he had abandoned. Abashed, he says to the king:

> If she, my liege, can make me know this clearly,
> I'll love her dearly, ever, ever dearly. (V.iii.315 – 16)

That is a terrible rhyme, and the repetition of "ever" makes the couplet even worse. Yet no one doubts that Shakespeare wrote those lines. It is the same playwright who, just a few moments before, had the King utter these rhymes to Bertram, when both he and the young man believe that Helena is dead:

> Our rash faults
> Make trivial price of serious things we have,

Not knowing them, until we know their grave.
Oft our displeasures, to ourselves unjust,
Destroy our friends and after weep their dust. (V.iii.60 – 64)

Those are mighty lines, and wise. They are utterly Shakespearean. Yet, as I said, Shakespeare wrote the banal lines too.

Those are from the same scene in the same play. To what dizzying multitude of authors would we assign the early history plays of King Henry the Sixth, the standard comedies of errors, the sprightly romantic comedies with a heroine at the center, the ghastly and farcical tragedy of *Titus Andronicus*, the nervous political plays on the reigns of Henry the Fourth and Henry the Fifth, the profound personal tragedies of *Hamlet* and *Othello*, the theological problem-plays *The Merchant of Venice* and *Measure for Measure*, the cynical social analyses of *Troilus and Cressida* and *Timon of Athens*, the lean and spare Roman plays of *Julius Caesar* and *Coriolanus*, the opulent *Antony and Cleopatra*, and the rich romances, of profound theological import, *Cymbeline*, *The Winter's Tale*, and *The Tempest*! We would have two Tudor historians, one much more accomplished than the other. We would have the bourgeois comedian. We would have the mighty aristocratic tragedian. We would have the clotted but sometimes fascinating author of farce. We would have the Pauline theologian. We would have the hanger-on of lawyers. We would have the classicist, always with Plutarch at his side. We would have the Christian romancer. And each single play too might break up into pieces. Yet we know that we have only one author, except for two plays for which we know that Shakespeare was a collaborator and not the principal, and it sometimes shows and it sometimes does not (*Henry VIII*, *The Two Noble Kinsmen*).

William Thackeray wrote, and drew the illustrations for, a couple of stories for children. Their language and their manner are nothing like what we get from the slashing and highly intellectual satirist in *Vanity Fair*. Cervantes was an unsuccessful playwright whose poetry gives little indication of the mighty many-spirited genius who wrote *Don Quixote*. Dante, in *La Vita Nuova*, wrote a markedly lame sonnet, "Love and the gentle heart are both one thing," in the middle of a work that for its potent drama is unlike anything anyone had written before. In that same *La Vita Nuova*, Dante often follows up his poems with what to our ears is most dreary and unnecessary identifications of their parts, thus: "This sonnet is divided into two parts. In the first part, I talk of love as it is in potentiality. In the second part, I talk of it as the potentiality is reduced to act. The second part begins: *Beauty appears.* The first part is also divided in two. In the first, I tell what the subject is wherein this potentiality exists. In the second, I tell how this subject and this potentiality are brought into being together." And so it goes on. It is not at all to our taste. It is not what we think a poet would do. But if we did not know better, we might suppose that a tedious commentator had obtruded himself upon the poet, and there would be learned disquisitions separating the one from the other. Why, we might see arguments, with evidence adduced, showing not only that Dante *did not* write the commentaries, but that Lapo di Gianni or some other of his contemporaries *did*.

Therefore there is no way, none, that anyone can justify on stylistic grounds a negative assertion, for example that Saint Paul *did not* write the letters to Timothy, or that John *did not* write the Apocalypse. People write in different ways for different purposes. They write in different ways at different times. Sometimes they are in a hurry. Sometimes they dictate a letter — Saint Paul seems to have done so: "I Tertius, who wrote this epistle, salute you in the Lord," says his secretary (Rom. 16:22). That alone is enough to make it impossible for us to say, for example, that Saint Peter did not write his epistles: "By Silvanus, a faithful brother unto you, as I suppose, I have written briefly" (1 Pt. 5:12). That is because the secretary will clean up the grammar of the person dictating, or will filter the dictation through his own sense of where sentences begin and end.

We can apply this reasoning to the twelve verses from John 7:53 to 8:11, which do not appear at all in some of the ancient manuscripts. Some people therefore have tried to justify their omission and have attempted to find some slight hitch in the style for support. I do not find any hitch at all, but a single word here or a pause there will not do, no more than the uncharacteristic repetition of the word "ever" in the lines that I have cited from *All's Well* shows that Shakespeare did not write them. It is not enough evidence for the weight of the assertion. It would be like trying to balance a pyramid upon its apex.

Meanwhile, the passage, which tells of the woman caught in adultery, is utterly convincing as an event from the life of Christ. It is another one of those moments that defies imitation. Recall when the Pharisees and the Herodians, enemies of one another but united in their enmity of Jesus, try to set a trap for Jesus by flattery, saying, "Master, we know that thou art true, and carest for no man: for thou regardest not the person of men, but teachest the way of God in truth: Is it lawful to give tribute to Caesar, or not?" (Mk. 12:14). Jesus sees through their words, "knowing their hypocrisy," that is, their play-acting (15). So he brings them on stage too: "Bring me a penny, that I may see it." Notice that he does not then say, "I see whose image is on this coin, and hence I draw this conclusion." He makes them say the words that will stick in their own throats. "Whose is this image and superscription?" he asks, "and they said unto him, Caesar's." Whereupon Jesus says, "Render to Caesar the things that are Caesar's, and to God the things that are God's" (15 – 17). That is no mere evasion, but a revelation which the statist Herodians on the one hand and the theocratic Pharisees on the other were not prepared to hear or to understand. But it is in accord with what Jesus says elsewhere: "My kingdom is not of this world" (Jn. 18:36).

Jesus is sitting down and teaching in the temple, and things seem calm enough, when suddenly the scribes and Pharisees bring to him a woman caught in adultery. It must have been a dramatic scene, because they say they caught her, as we say, in flagrante delicto. "Now Moses in the law," they say, "commanded us, that such should be stoned: but what sayest thou?" (Jn. 8:5). The pronoun is emphatic. We might say it this way in English: "But you, what do you say about it?"

Again they seek to hem him on both sides. If he agrees, he will appear subordinate to them, and he will seem to have enjoined upon them an act of capital punishment, forbidden to them by their Roman overlords: "It is not lawful for us to put any man to death," they say to Pilate, when Pilate obviously wants no part of dealing with Jewish theological controversies (18:31). Given the many crimes for which Moses prescribed the punishment of death, the enemies of Jesus can only be referring to Roman law. "We have no king but Caesar," they say, either lying so as to keep on the lee side of Roman relations with the Jews, or condemning themselves of apostasy by their own words (19:15). But if Jesus does not agree that the woman should be put to death, he will appear to have treated the law of Moses with contempt, and in the very temple itself.

At this point "Jesus stooped down, and with his finger wrote on the ground" (8:6). It is another of those things that an eyewitness remembers, an apparently irrelevant detail of a scene that strikes the mind and remains there, with power to bring back to immediacy the whole drama. Nevertheless, we are within our rights to ask what Jesus is doing here. John is too chaste to say. If he were making it up, he would say something, and in fact some over-helpful copyist in one manuscript has supplied a suggestion, that Jesus was writing down their sins. Perhaps he was. Perhaps he was not. We do not know. Maybe it was the words *le'olam chasdo*, *his mercy is forever* (cf. Ps. 118:1). Maybe it was the words *'ahabta le-re'aka kamoka, thou shalt love thy neighbor as thyself* (cf. Lev. 19:18). Maybe it was the words that David wrote, when he had been caught in adultery with Bathsheba: *channeni Elohim ke-chasdeka, Be gracious to me, O Lord, like unto thy mercy* (cf. Ps. 51:1). Perhaps in glory we will be given to know what it was. It is the only time in the gospels that Jesus is shown as writing something. I suppose, whatever it was, it was something that the accusers of the woman should have known.

Jesus allows them to go on, as the tension mounts. Then he *got up from his stooping* (Greek *anekypsen*) and said to them, "He that is without sin among you, let him first cast a stone at her" (Jn. 8:7). Then he stoops down again and resumes his writing on the ground.

To catch the full power of what Jesus says here, we should notice something that comes across in Greek and Hebrew but not in English. In John's Greek, the man *without sin* is *anamartetos*, someone without *hamartia, sin*. The word for sin comes from archery: it is to miss the mark, to shoot the arrow awry. The same sort of metaphor underlies the Hebrew verb *chata*, *to sin*, meaning also that you err, you miss your way, you go wide of the mark. Who then would be more fit to cast the first stone at the sinful woman, *than one whose aim has always been true?*

But we know that our aim is not true. The people know it. That is why they leave, quietly, one by one, from the eldest to the least. They have not trapped Jesus in their play. Jesus has convicted them in his play. And again he *got up from stooping* (Greek *anakypsas*), and now he brings the woman into the play. He does not at first interpret for her what has happened. He asks her for her interpretation: "Woman, where are those thine accusers? hath no man condemned thee?" (8:10).

Man, ever quick to condemn, so long as it is not himself! The woman, who through the whole scene has made no plea, no excuse, replies simply, "No man, Lord." To which Jesus replies, "Neither do I condemn thee: go, and sin no more" (11). It is as if he had said, "Go, and wander no more from the way." He does not specify the wandering. He does not do what elsewhere he shows himself quite willing to do, to name our shameful deeds. He simply says, "Go, and sin no more." He might as well have said, "Come, follow the way."

All of that, in a few lines of text. As I have said, it defies imitation.

ON DAMNING BOTH WAYS

The leaders of the Jews were constantly pressing Jesus to give them a *sign*. The word in Hebrew, *'owth*, is regularly used to denote a wonder, a miraculous token of the action of God. So when the king Hezekiah was sick unto death, he prayed to the Lord to spare him for yet awhile, and the Lord sent Isaiah to him to say, "I will add unto thy days fifteen years" (2 Kg. 20:6). Hezekiah, not quite sure of the matter, asked Isaiah for a sign, and Isaiah said, "This sign shalt thou have of the Lord," and he let Hezekiah choose whether the shadow of the sun on the sundial should advance or retreat ten degrees. "And Hezekiah answered, It is a light thing for the shadow to go down ten degrees: nay, but let the shadow return backward ten degrees," and Isaiah cried unto the Lord, and so it happened as Hezekiah had asked (9 – 11).

"What sign shewest thou to us," say the Jews, when Jesus had whipped the moneychangers in the temple, "seeing that thou doest these things?" (Jn. 2:18). So also when he had cast a demon out of a man, and the Pharisees said that he did it in the name of Beelzebub. "Master, we would see a sign from thee," they say, not accepting the sign he had already performed before their eyes (Mt. 12:38). But Jesus replies, "An evil and adulterous generation seeketh after a sign; and there shall no sign be given to it, but the sign of the prophet Jonas" (39). He is foretelling his resurrection from the dead, and that is why, if you go to the Sistine Chapel in Rome, you will see that Michelangelo has situated his colossal painting of Jonah being spat forth by the whale above the apse, whose wall he would eventually cover with a painting of the final judgment and the resurrection of the flesh.

Jesus performed signs all the time, and the people did not read them. He does not simply say that only those who believe will see the signs. He sometimes makes the sign so that people will believe. So it was when he raised Lazarus from the dead: "that they may believe," he prays to the Father, "that thou hast sent me" (Jn. 11:42). So it was when he cured the paralytic: "But that ye may know that the Son of man hath power on earth to forgive sins, (he saith to the sick of the palsy,) I say unto thee, Arise, and take up thy bed, and go thy way into thine house" (Mk. 2:10 – 11). All the miracles of Jesus mean something. They are true signs: he does not put forth his power as a sideshow. We understand by them that he is who he says he is, and when we believe that he is the Son of God, we understand them all the more. Light brings on light.

But suppose someone says that there is no proof that Jesus is the Son of God. He wants a sign. We have plenty of signs to give him. We give him the miracles that Jesus performed. Then he says that those miracles could not have happened, but that the accounts were made up by the disciples. And so we are damned both ways. He demands a miracle, and when we give him a miracle, he will not accept it, because it is a miracle, and he says that miracles are impossible. He will say that the history of the world is full of charlatans and sleight-of-hand artists. We then beg him to name for us a single charlatan or sleight-of-hand artist who did the things Jesus is reported to have done, *and who said the things that Jesus said*, things that, as I have noted, make the wisest moralist, a Lao-Tzu or Emerson or Epictetus, sound like a garrulous peddler of platitudes by comparison. Then he may concede that Jesus was a great teacher. But when we beg him to notice that much of what Jesus taught was about *who he is*, they say that he was mistaken about that, or that his disciples made it up afterwards. So Jesus is a great teacher, and almost in the same breath he is a dupe; or the apostles are the slow addle-pated creatures they appear to be in the gospels, and almost in the same breath they are the crafters of a conspiracy unparalleled for its diabolical genius. What do people want? The apostles are illiterate and credulous laborers, and before the sentence is over they possess the strategic powers of Hannibal and the intellectual cunning of Socrates. We are damned both ways.

We see the same phenomenon at work when people say that the gospels of Matthew and Luke must have been written after the destruction of Jerusalem in the year 70, because Jesus is obviously portrayed as foretelling it, in apocalyptic terms (Mt. 24, Lk. 21). Here I must confess complete astonishment. It required no man of keen insight into human history to foretell that the Romans would finally lose patience with the Jews and raze their capital to the ground! The Romans had been putting down rebellions there for a long time, and in the time of Jesus relations between them and the Jews were clearly tense, at best. The Barabbas whom Pontius Pilate released instead of Jesus was "a robber," says John (23:19), using a word that suggests not petty thievery but sacking and plundering. Luke puts it more strongly: Barabbas "for a certain sedition made in the city, and for murder, was cast into prison" (Lk. 23:19). Caiaphas the high priest says that it would be better for one innocent man to die than for the whole people to perish, meaning that they must do what they can to keep the Romans from destroying them (Jn. 11:50). Why then must we think that the Son of God could not do what an ordinary political observer could do?

Meanwhile, if Jesus's predictions in Matthew and Luke "prove" that those gospels were written after Jerusalem was destroyed, why does not the glaring omission of that prediction not "prove" that the gospel of John was written *before* Jerusalem was destroyed? The sword cuts both ways. Of course, the answer to the problem is that there is no problem to answer. A man who could foretell his resurrection from the dead, and who could heal the blind and cure the sick, could well make a political prediction. Which, after all, is easier? To say, "The Romans will eventually lay waste to this whole city," or, "Take up thy bed, and go thy way"?

Someone may say that Matthew's account of that destruction, and of the end times generally, owes much to the Jewish form of literature called "apocalyptic," such as we find in the apocryphal book, 4 Esdras. I do not doubt it. I have, after all, claimed that Jesus is composing traditional Semitic poetry in the Beatitudes and the Lord's Prayer. But again, if apocalyptic was available to Matthew, it was available to Jesus, and it is Jesus, not Matthew, who is otherwise the poet.

Then we have Saint Luke. It is not in dispute that Luke, "the beloved physician" (Col. 4:14), accompanied Saint Paul on his later journeys, and we see as much in the Acts of the Apostles, when Luke so often uses the first person plural pronoun: "And after he had seen the vision, immediately we endeavored to go into Macedonia" (Acts 16:10). Now, Acts ends with Saint Paul still alive and in Rome: "And Paul dwelt two whole years in his own hired house, and received all that came in unto him, Preaching the kingdom of God, and teaching those things which concern the Lord Jesus Christ, with all confidence, no man forbidding him" (Acts 28:30–31). Paul is still awaiting judgment by Caesar.

What is missing here is any account of Paul's martyrdom. People acknowledge that Saint Luke is a fine writer, with a flair for setting a dramatic scene: think of his account of the martyrdom of Saint Stephen (Acts 7), witnessed by Saint Paul, who was one of the movers behind Stephen's condemnation. If Luke is writing as late as so many commentators say, where is the climax to his story? So we are to believe that the same writer *does include* Jesus's prophecy of the destruction of Jerusalem in 70, because it had already happened, but he *does not include* the martyrdom of his friend and fellow evangelist Paul, even though that happened *before* Jerusalem was destroyed? Again, the answer to the problem is to assert that there is no problem. Saint Luke does not tell us that Paul was put to death, because Paul had not yet been put to death. His gospel, written before his sequel Acts, has Jesus foretell the calamity that would befall Jerusalem, because Jesus in fact did that. He foretold it.

The same damning both ways applies when people deny that the apostle John is the one who wrote the Apocalypse. If, granting their own assumptions, Luke and Matthew put apocalyptic description on the lips of Jesus, because apocalypse was in the air, why cannot John put apocalyptic description on his own lips, because apocalypse is in the air? Or, if Jesus spoke in apocalyptic terms, setting aside his more ordinary subjects of discourse, why could not John do the same? But then, what precisely are our grounds for insisting that John set out to write in the apocalyptic vein, as a deliberate and wholly human choice? Supposing that it was such a choice, then we have no grounds for saying, on the grounds of difference in subject matter and treatment, that Revelation could not have been written by the author of the gospel. If I ever write an apocalyptic story, I assure my readers now that its language and subject will have little in common with those of this book on Saint John's prologue. But *why should we suppose that it was a choice?* We are told otherwise. We are told it was a vision. No doubt that vision might well be impressed upon the mind of John in a way that called up the language and the symbolism of the apocalyptic authors before him. If I ever have an apocalyptic vision, I assure my readers now that I will write about it in English, and that the ways of English literature and of English translations of the book of Revelation will have been in my mind when God imparts the vision. In short, perhaps John wrote the Apocalypse of John in the way he did because that in fact was how the Apocalypse appeared to John.

ON FLOWER CHILDREN AND DISORGANIZATION

The more closely I have examined the gospel of John, the more does any romantic notion of spontaneous effusions of some religious "spirit" fade from credibility. The gospel is organized. The very prologue is organized.

If you lived in England or Scotland during the years when the great machine of industry was first set into motion, and men who had once been fully alive were reduced to factory hands, you might well cast a longing eye toward what you supposed would be a life closer to "nature," so long as you had somebody come in to do your laundry. "Simplify, simplify," said Thoreau, not acknowledging that the deliberately chosen simplicity of the romantic rests upon a network of social relationships, bound by mutual obligations, and structured in a hierarchy of authority and obedience. Look into the ways of American Indians, and you find a veritable mesh of demands and taboos, rules for inheritance, rules for marriage, rules for bringing up children, rules for ushering boys into the duties of manhood, initiation rites, special chants for the shaman to chant for each disease; you never find disorganization or mere license, and you never will. That is not how mankind is.

We see a clear base of organization already in the words and the deeds of Jesus. It is Jesus, unmistakably, who singled out twelve men for special duties, the twelve apostles. This is not in dispute. Why twelve, and not eleven or thirteen? It is because Jesus is re-establishing the twelve tribes of Israel. But if that is so, then he has in mind quite an organization. Think of the moment when he gives Simon the son of Jonah an official name: "And I say unto thee, That thou art Peter, and upon this rock I will build my church" (Mt. 16:18). Those who say that Jesus was just a moral visionary who never intended to found anything so bulky and lumpy and earthy as a *church* must deal then with these words. They deal with them by denying that Jesus ever said them. When you press them for evidence, they say that Jesus would not have said them, because he was just a moral visionary who never intended to found anything so bulky and lumpy and so forth. The dog chases his tail.

If we consider either the Hebrew that might underlie Jesus's words to Peter, or the Greek in which Matthew expresses them, we see organization everywhere. The Hebrew for *build* is *banah*, and it suggests at its root the *building up of a family*: "Behold my maid Bilhah, go in unto her," says the still childless Rachel to Jacob, "and she shall bear upon my knees, that I may also *have children* by her" (Gen. 30:3; Hebrew *ibbaneh*). There are several words that might do for *church*; all of them imply organization. The most likely one, given Jesus's commands to the disciples to go forth and preach, is *qahal, assembly, convocation,* especially for religious purposes. "The heavens shall praise thy wonders, O Lord," sings Ethan the Ezrahite, "thy faithfulness also in the *congregation of the saints*" (Ps. 89:5; Hebrew *qahal qedoshim*). It is translated as *synagoge* in the Septuagint. Is it not obvious from everything that Jesus has had to say about the Law and the temple that establishing a new synagogue, that is, a new congregation, built upon a new foundation, his own self, is exactly what he is about?

The Greek for *I shall build* — and it is powerfully suggestive that Jesus gives Simon a Greek name rather than a Hebrew or Aramaic name — in the verse from Matthew is *oikodomeso*, from the common noun *oîkos*, *house*, and the verb *demein*, *to build*, *to construct* (cf. Latin *domus*, *house*; English *timber*). We must not think of the structure of stone or wood where a person sleeps at night after coming home from work. The house is an organization, stretching backward and forward in time: it is a *household*. So the *master of the house* is the *oikodespotes* (cf. English *despot*), and the *steward* is the *oikonomos*, the *manager of the household laws* (cf. English *economy*). What Jesus will build upon the rock of Peter is his *ekklesia*. That too is a common Greek word, with many social applications, all of them suggesting a high order of organization, as in the assembly or *ekklesia* of Athens, where things would be up for *debating* (Greek *ekklesiazein*), by any *speaker at the assembly* (Greek *ekklesiastes*). It is not the only time the word *ekklesia* translates what Jesus has said. We find it elsewhere in Matthew, uncontroversially, where Jesus gives directions regarding disputes (18 : 17). But what really is powerful about it is the verb it expresses: *ekkalein*, *to call forth*. So Saint Paul reminds the Galatians of what they are supposed to be: "I marvel that ye are so soon removed from him that *called* you into the grace of Christ" (Gal. 1 : 6; Greek *kalesantos*).

So Jesus, who preaches always and commands the disciples to preach, whose parables are filled with building up households and managing them, who says that he will build a new temple, and who calls people into a new assembly, is to be made into a flower child, who had no notion of building anything that would last longer than a parade. That makes no sense. "Heaven and earth shall pass away," he says, "but my words shall not pass away" (Mk. 13 : 31).

It is simply a matter of human nature that we *organize* what we do, and the more important the thing is, the more quickly and clearly we form it into an organization. Saint Paul's metaphor of the body implies organization and hierarchy: "And God hath set some in the church, first apostles, secondarily prophets, thirdly teachers, after that miracles, then gifts of healings, helps, governments, diversities of tongues" (1 Cor. 12 : 28). Christ is not the head of a bowl of emotional jelly. So when critics attribute a late date to this or that writing of the New Testament, saying that it bespeaks a degree of organization that would have required many decades for the church to form, I wonder if they have ever been part of a bowling league or a chess club, let alone something as powerful and danger-ridden as the gathering of the first Christians.

There is, then, nothing, absolutely nothing, that requires us to believe that the book of Revelation, wherein John writes "to the seven churches which are in Asia" (Rev. 1:4), must be very late, just because there are organizations there, nor is there any reason why the Saint Paul who insists upon order and hierarchy in the body should not also, in the letters to his beloved Timothy the bishop, give advice on the sensible management of the household that is the church. Once we give up our own odd inclinations against order and authority, and our odd romantic assumptions regarding what should count as genuine religious impulses, the problems vanish.

Conclusion

WHO IS THE THEOLOGIAN?
Who is the man who can tell us about the *Logos Theou,*
the Word of God?

If we believe that the word of God is the word of God, and not just human words about God, and if we believe that Jesus Christ is the Word that was with God from the beginning, for he himself was God, then the theologian is one who has delved most deeply into the Word and the words, drawing nearer and nearer to Christ. He heeds the words of Saint Peter, as John reports them to us, when so many of those who followed Jesus drew away from him, because they did not understand what he meant when he said he was the living bread come down from heaven. "To whom shall we go?" said Peter. "Thou hast the words of eternal life" (Jn. 6:68).

The theologian is not in the same position as is the physicist or even the historian. The physicist studies matter as matter, outside of himself. If he sins against his brother, still the hydrogen atom has one electron and not two. The historian may be involved with his subject in a human way, just to understand better the ways of men on their own terms. Still, Booth fired the shot in Ford's Theater, and Lincoln fell. But one who wishes to say things about God and his Anointed One cannot treat the matter in that way, because we are in the realm of personhood here, the ultimate Person, who calls to each man as a person, saying, "Seek my face" (Ps. 27:8). The theologian cannot elude the call. God is not a respecter of pretended impersonality.

The theologian should attempt to treat as intelligently as possible the material and historical circumstances surrounding the person of Jesus and his life, but ultimately he must face the question that Jesus posed to the apostles: "But whom say ye that I am?" (Mt. 16:15). And here he must answer. He may wrap himself around with the fat of sentimentality, and pose as someone who feels deeply for the man who was so poorly understood by the religious people of his time. I suspect, however, that they who crucified him understood him better than the sentimentalist does. The question, in any case, is not whether Jesus deserves our esteem. To hell with human esteem. The question is whether we look to him as our savior, even if it means being nailed to a tree beside him.

135

If the answer to that question is yes, if we confess that Jesus is Lord, then despite our stupidities, our cowardice, our wickedness, and our sad attempts to be pure in heart for a single hour, we cannot treat of Jesus and the gospels as we treat of anyone or anything else in the world. We must come to know *him*. The theologian is the person who knows Jesus. The theologian is the person who prays, who obeys even if by fits and starts the invaluable commandments that Jesus gives to us as a grace, and who then attains what Jesus has promised him: light.

It is a commonplace of scholastic theology that love follows upon knowledge. The intellect sees what is good, and the will, in obedience, follows upon the vision, and that desire is what we call love. But love, says Richard of Saint Victor, opens us up to see. Where there is love, he says, there is an eye for seeing. If I have said anything in this book that places a stumbling stone between any soul and the Lord, I pray that the Lord will not hold it against me, because I intended no such thing; and I beg such a soul to set the book aside and pray. If I have said anything that removes a stumbling stone between any soul and the Lord, it is none of my doing but his, the Lord's. And I say with the thief, "Lord, remember me when thou comest into thy kingdom" (Lk. 23:42).

Pearls of Price

O Word that goest forth on high
    From God's own depths eternally,
And in these latter days wast born
    For succor to a world forlorn:
Pour light upon us from above,
    And fire our hearts with ardent love,
That, as we hear thy truth today,
    All wrong desires may burn away.
      — *Verbum supernum prodiens*, 7th c.

God of God, Light of Light,
Lo, he abhors not the Virgin's womb;
Very God, begotten, not created.
      — *Adeste fideles*, 18th c.,
      trans. Frederick Oakeley

Veiled in flesh the Godhead see,
    Hail, the incarnate Deity,
Pleased as man with man to dwell,
    Jesus, our Immanuel.
      — Charles Wesley
    "Hark, the Herald Angels Sing," 1739

Glorious now behold him arise,
King, and God, and Sacrifice;
Heaven sings Alleluia,
Alleluia the earth replies.
      — John Henry Hopkins
    "We Three Kings," 1857

The glory of these forty days
We celebrate with songs of praise,
For Christ, by whom all things were made,
Himself has fasted and has prayed.
      — *Clarum decus ieiunii*, 6th c.,
      trans. Maurice F. Bell, 1906

The royal banners forward go,
The cross shines forth in mystic glow
Where he, as man, who gave man breath,
Now bows beneath the yoke of death.

> — Prudentius
> *Vexilla regis prodeunt*, 569

Rise from the grave now, O Lord,
    who art author of life and creation.
Treading the pathway of death,
    life thou bestowest on man.

> — Venantius Fortunatus, 530 – 609
> *Salva festa dies*

O sons and daughters, let us sing!
The King of heaven, the glorious King,
O'er death today rose triumphing.

> — Jean Tisserand
> *O filii et filiae*, 15th c.,
> trans. John Mason Neale, 1852

O Light of all the earth,
    Thy children wait for thee!
Come to thy temples here,
    That we, from sin set free,
Before thy Father's face
    May all presented be!

> — John Ellerton
> "Hail to the Lord Who Comes," 1880

But silent yet the mother blest
    Of the yet silent Word,
And pondering all things in her heart,
    With speechless praise adored.

> — Jean Baptiste De Santeuil, 1680,
> trans. Edward Caswall, 1849

Rank on rank the host of heaven
Spreads its vanguard on the way,
As the Light of Light descendeth
From the realms of endless day,
That the powers of hell may vanish
As the darkness clears away.

— *Sigesato pasa sarx broteia,*
trans. Gerard Moultrie, 1864

Only-begotten, Word of God eternal,
  Lord of creation, merciful and mighty,
Hear now thy servants, when their joyful voices
  Rise to thy presence.

— *Christe cunctorum Dominator alme,*
9th c., trans. Maxwell J. Blacker, 1884

He came, God's Word to the world below,
And round him there did gather
A band who found that this teacher to know
Was even to know the Father.

— Percy Dearmer, 1928

Behold the Lamb of God!
All hail, incarnate Word,
Thou everlasting Lord,
Savior most blest;
Fill us with love that never faints,
Grant us with all thy blessed saints
Eternal rest.

— Matthew Bridges, 1848

Crown him the Son of God
Before the worlds began,
And ye, who tread where he hath trod,
Crown him the Son of man;
Who every grief hath known
That wrings the human breast,
And takes and bears them for his own,
That all in him may rest.

    — Matthew Bridges
"Crown Him with Many Crowns," 1851

All praise to thee, for thou, O King divine,
Didst yield the glory that of right was thine,
That in our darkened hearts thy grace might shine.
    — F. Bland Tucker, 1938

The Church's one foundation
Is Jesus Christ her Lord;
She is his new creation,
By water and the word:
From heaven he came and sought her
To be his holy bride;
With his own blood he bought her,
And for her life he died.

    — Samuel John Stone, 1866

There God forever sitteth,
Himself of all the crown;
The Lamb, the Light that shineth
And never goeth down.

    — George C. Martin
"O Heavenly Jerusalem," 1892

And there no sun was needed,
Nor moon to shine by night,
God's glory did enlighten all,
The Lamb himself the light.

    — Godfrey Thring
"I Heard a Sound of Voices," 1886

O higher than the cherubim,
More glorious than the seraphim,
Lead their praises, Alleluia!
Thou bearer of the eternal Word,
Most gracious, magnify the Lord, Alleluia!

       — Athelstan Riley
       "Ye Watchers and Ye Holy Ones," 1909

[I believe] in one Lord Jesus Christ,
the only-begotten Son of God;
begotten of the Father before all worlds,
God of God, Light of Light, Very God of Very God,
begotten, not made, being of one substance with the Father;
by whom all things were made.

       — From the Nicene Creed

Let sighing cease and woe,
God from on high hath heard,
Heaven's gate is opening wide, and lo!
The long-expected Word.

       — Charles Coffin, 1676 – 1749
       Iam desinant suspiria,
       trans. W. J. Blew

This day the first of days was made,
When God in light the world arrayed;
Or when his Word arose again,
And, conquering death, gave life to men.

       — Saint Gregory the Great, 6th c.
       Primo dierum omnium,
       trans. Robert Bridges

O Christ, who art the Light and Day,
Thou drivest darksome night away!
We know thee as the Light of light,
Illuminating mortal sight.

       — Latin, 7th c.
       Christe qui lux es et dies,
       trans. W. J. Copeland

At the Lamb's high feast we sing
Praise to our victorious King:
Who hath washed us in the tide
Flowing from his pierced side.

> — R. Campbell, 1814 – 1868,
> based on *Ad regias Agni dapes*

O Christ, our hope, our hearts' desire,
   Redemption's only spring;
Creator of the world art thou,
   Its Savior and its King.

> — Latin, 8th c.
> *Jesu nostra redemptio,*
> trans. J. Chandler

Light, sole and one, we thee confess,
With triple praise we rightly bless;
Alpha and Omega we own,
With every spirit round thy throne.

> — Latin, 10th c.
> *Adesto, sancta Trinitas,*
> trans. John Mason Neale

Most ancient of all mysteries,
   Before thy throne we lie;
Have mercy now, most merciful,
   Most holy Trinity.
When heaven and earth were yet unmade,
   When time was yet unknown,
Thou in thy bliss and majesty
   Didst live and love alone.

> — Frederick W. Faber, 1814 – 1868
> "Have Mercy on Us, God Most High"

O Word immortal of eternal God,
Only-begotten of the only Source,
For our salvation stooping to the course
Of human life, and born of Mary's blood. . .
Save us, O Christ our God, for thou hast died
To save thy people to the uttermost,
And dying tramplest death in victory;
One of the ever blessed Trinity,
In equal honor with the Holy Ghost,
And with the eternal Father glorified.

> — Justinian, 483 – 565
> *Ho monogenes Hyios,*
> trans. Thomas Alexander Lacey

"Worthy the Lamb that died," they cry,
　"to be exalted thus";
"Worthy the Lamb," our lips reply,
　"for he was slain for us."

> — Isaac Watts, 1674 – 1748
> "Come, Let Us Join Our Cheerful Songs"

Jesu, Deliverer,
　near to us be;
Soothe thou my voyaging
　over life's sea.
Thou, when the storm of death
　roars, sweeping by,
Whisper, O Truth of Truth,
　"Peace! It is I."

> — Anatolius, 8th c.
> *Zopheras trikymias,*
> trans. John Mason Neale

I lay my sins on Jesus,
The spotless Lamb of God;
He bears them all, and frees us
From the accursed load.
I bring my guilt to Jesus,
To wash my crimson stains
White in his Blood most precious,
Till not a spot remains.

— Horatio Bonar, 1808 – 1889

ABOUT THE AUTHOR

ANTHONY ESOLEN is a professor of humanities, and writer in residence, at Magdalen College of the Liberal Arts. He has written or translated twenty-five books, on language, literature, culture, and the Christian faith, including a three-volume translation and edition of Dante's *Divine Comedy*, and, most recently, his own book-length poem *The Hundredfold: Songs for the Lord*. He lives in Warner, New Hampshire, with his wife Debra and their two children, Jessica and David.

CPSIA information can be obtained
at www.ICGtesting.com
Printed in the USA
BVHW030201200122
626689BV00010B/71/J

9 781621 387985